'Anyone who has idly fingered a roll of Sellotape or flipped a beermat back and forth … will enjoy Connor on the joy of fidgeting.' *New Statesman*

'Applies the techniques of literary theory to stuff … enchanting' *Independent*

'Who would have thought that fishing at the back of a desk drawer or the bottom of a handbag could reel in such treasures? Thanks to this book, fidgeting will be a far more thoughtful occupation in the future.' Daniel Miller

'The familiar becomes strange as un-thought-out everyday items are examined in such a way that they become magical.' *Times Higher Education*

'Turns a nimble wit and a fresh eye to bags, batteries and buttons' *Scotland on Sunday*

'An entertaining history of everyday objects and personal possessions' *Bookseller*

D0280156

STEVEN CONNOR is Grace 2 Professor of English in the University of Cambridge. He is the author of many academic books (on subjects ranging from the English novel to ventriloquism, air, skin, flies and sport) and contributes regularly to print media and radio.

Paraphernalia

The Curious Lives of Magical Things

Steven Connor

PROFILE BOOKS

This paperback edition published in 2013

First published in Great Britain in 2011 by
PROFILE BOOKS LTD
3A Exmouth House
Pine Street, Exmouth Market
London ECIR OJH
www.profilebooks.com

Copyright © Steven Connor, 2011, 2013

1 3 5 7 9 10 8 6 4 2

Artwork by Richard Green
Designed by Geoff Green Book Design, Cambridge
Typeset in Adobe Caslon by MacGuru Ltd
info@macguru.org.uk
Printed and bound in Great Britain by CPI Group (UK) Ltd, Croydon CRO 4YY

The moral right of the author has been asserted.

A CIP catalogue record for this book is available from the British Library.

ISBN 978 1 84668 271 1
eISBN 978 1 84765 282 9

Contents

Introduction: Speaking of Objects

Magical Things

Waiting in Dublin airport once, in the state of tipsily philosophical bliss that is common with me in airports, I saw a baby aged about nine months sitting at its parents' feet. The baby was entirely absorbed in a game that involved stretching and releasing the strap of its mother's handbag, while sliding the buckle up and down its length. At one point, its mother reached down and carelessly handed it a piece of muffin to eat. The baby looked from the muffin to the handbag, seemingly weighing the chances of it being able to play some useful part in its push-me-pull-you investigation. After a couple of puzzled moments, the muffin was thrown aside and the baby resumed its researches. I had never seen such absorption and intentness, and have never forgotten it. The baby was simultaneously concentrated and abandoned, utterly in and at the same time entirely out of this world. I thought I had seen something amazing:

a creature coming into being in its very capacity to leave itself behind in the ecstasy of play.

What was more amazing was that this miracle of animation came into being through something seemingly simple and inanimate. For this is how we usually think of things such as bags – as just there, inert, without will or consciousness. When we speak of an object – from *ob-*, opposite or against, and *–iacere*, to throw – our word evokes something that is thrown or thrust up against us. The word 'object' seems to assert the existence of that which stands apart, and has no part of us.

But this book is about a different kind of object, or one experienced in a different kind of way, that, like the enigmatic bag under such intent investigation in the airport, seems to escape its own finitude, its dourly objectish being-there, to go beyond, or spill to the side of, what it merely is or does. I am going to call this kind of thing a magical object. One way of putting this is to say that such objects are invested with powers, associations and significances, that they are therefore not just docile things, but signs, showings, epiphanies. The meditations on objects I offer here will indeed often suggest that they can be seen as what in the fifteenth and sixteenth centuries in Europe would have been called 'emblems', allegories of human life, implying pocket homilies on love, time, hope, error, striving and death. As such, they give us work to do as well as being merely available for us to work on. And yet, their power comes entirely from us.

But this should not be taken to imply that these are fundamentally neutral or inert objects that we have merely tricked up with symbolic significance or buttered with 'sentimental value'. Objects often have what J. J. Gibson calls 'affordance', meaning that they seem to hold out certain very specific kinds of physical invitation to us, often involving an angle of approach or physical address.[1] A teacup asks to be picked up by the handle; a brandy glass invites one to cradle it, tender as a dove, from underneath; a shoe hints pointedly at a particular kind of toe-first, Cinderella insertion; a table spreads its flat expanse generously for banquet or billiards; a chair irresistibly proposes that one lower oneself into it backwards. Such objects seem to have us, or certain parts of us, imaged in them. The affordances of objects means that they are not merely externally loaded with associations and connotations, but that we find ourselves implicated in, or apprehended by, them. We act in accordance with the affordances of objects. Things are taken up with, preoccupied by, us.

The function of a highly specialised piece of equipment is usually inscribed clearly in its form; it has to be exactly the way it is and not some other way because it is *for* one particular kind of thing. What is more, it may seem to require of us a certain kind of highly specific posture or stylised movement. But magical objects seem in some respect not to be merely given in this way. It is not that they are awkward, enigmatic or non-compliant. Rather it is that they seem to offer richer and more indeterminate kinds of affordance, making them seem in various ways excessive to their ordinary or assigned uses. Magical things all do more, and mean more than they might be supposed to. A ball is a magical object because its affordances, its ways of proposing itself for use, are at once so irresistible and yet also so seemingly open. The more common an object is, the more various the uses it will propose, or make possible. That is why so many of the magical objects I discuss here are adapted to uses different from those for which they were ostensibly devised. Magical objects in this sense are always playthings, things that seem not to give some specific instruction as to their use, like the labels saying 'eat me' and 'drink me' on objects in Wonderland, but rather seem to say, 'play with me: try to make out what I might be good for'. Magical things invite a kind of practical *rêverie*, a kind of floating but intent circling through or playing with possibilities, a following out of their implied reach. Magical objects are such stuff as dreams are made on. They afford reflection on their affordances.

So the essence of what I am going to call a magical thing is that it is more than a mere thing. We can do whatever we like to things, but magical things are things that we allow and expect to do things back to us. Magical things surpass themselves, in allowing us to increment or surpass ourselves with them. They are things, as we say, to be *conjured with*, though their magic is done on ourselves rather than on others. Such objects have the powers to arouse, absorb, steady, seduce, disturb, soothe, succour and drug. If they seem to have a life of their own, it is a life that we give them, and give back to ourselves through them.

Fidgetables and forget-me-nots

Many of the objects with which I shall be so earnestly toying in this book are also *fidgetables*, things that hold out the possibility of being fiddled with – buttons, elastic bands, pins, sticky tape, glasses. Fidgeting expresses our oddly intimate relationship to objects. Fidgeting always requires an object, something to fidget with, even if it is only with oneself. Indeed, the urge to fidget might almost be put down to the need for or lack of some object, and the casting about for and taking up of some substitute for that object. Without some kind of object to fidget with (a cigarette, a biro, a slip of paper, a lock of hair), one becomes fidgety.

But, even though we may have favourite fidgetables, fidgeting is never satisfied with any particular object. This is because fidgeting is itself a process of searching for what might be called the ideal object. I mean by this something that is at once part of the world, something that can be owned and kept and fixed in place and relied upon to stay put, in all the usual ways that objects can – and yet also resembles me, in all my fugitive variability, all my ways of being beside, and taking leave of, myself. The philosopher and historian of science Gaston Bachelard has evoked, as one avatar of this kind of object, what he calls the dream of an ideal paste. The ideal paste (of which snow, ice cream, mashed potato, putty, playdough and potter's clay, all of them generalised kinds of *stuff*, are versions) is infinitely malleable, while yet never becoming entirely liquid, for at that point it would begin to escape me. The ideal object resists me, while yet also yielding; yields, while never simply giving way before me.[2] It is capable of being deformed beyond recognition while yet persisting in itself. It is in fact like me, or the way I take myself to be, in being infinitely variable while yet miraculously remaining the same. It is capable of being put maximally to work, which is to say, maximally in play. We play with such objects as we do with all playthings, for an entirely circular reason – namely, to find out how much play (in the sense of give, stretch or variability) they may be found to pos-sess. Sometimes, the action of taking an object to its limits will result in its being tested to destruction. Eventually, the paper clip snaps. Perhaps all play has at its horizon the death of the plaything. When we put something to work, we use it for a particular purpose. In play, we seek not so much to use things as to *use them up*. The point of putting things into play may be to play them out, to see how far they go, how far we can go with the open totality of their affordances. And, at the same time, we put ourselves into play, we use these objects to play with ourselves, even to toy with our own play, seeking its possibilities and limits.

What is more, it can seem as though, when we play with an object, we are also in part playing with the idea of the object, as well as the particular example of it that we may have to hand. Certainly, the objects I am going to write about tend to be generic rather than particular. Though I have found it very difficult to write about the things I write about here without actually having examples of them physically to hand as well as in mind, what I have been trying to get at in each case has usually been what might be called the specificity of the generic – just what it is about bags or batteries or rubber bands in general that makes each one itself. My point is not to try to get a particular, favoured specimen to stand out from the background of all bags, but rather to get particular things to open up about how they open on to all the other examples of the things in question of which we have had experience. It occurs to me that I might very well therefore have called this book *Indefinite articles*, since all the things with which it deals are more aptly designated by the word 'a' than by the pinpointing definite article 'the'. If I write about a rubber band, it is as an example of rubber bands in general, an example of the way in which each individual rubber band will always be such an example.

What is more, this generality is a loose or non-finite generality. My quarry is not in The Rubber Band, the Band of Bands, the Platonic essence, or mother-idea that precedes and programmes all mundane instances of rubber bands. Rather, I am interested in the way in which every single example of a rubber band seems to invoke and participate in the ongoing totality of all the other rubber bands we have met and that there might yet be for us.

What is more, I will be interested in the sorts of general forms and possibilities that ordinary objects are keyed into – the many different kinds of thing we can mean by a 'card' (postcards, playing cards, credit cards), for example, or the many different functions that different kinds of plugs can perform, or the many actions of combing, riddling and sieving in which combs seem to be implicated. These objects are not just put to different uses, they generate anthologies or repertoires of allied forms.

Some of the magical objects about which I write have been around for a very long time, and others are much newer. But all of them are strangely anachronistic. One of the ways in which we set ourselves over against things is in the belief that we are threaded through and through with time. We feel ourselves to be the subjects of time, whereas things seem merely subject to it. Beings like us emerge, evolve and die, because, we persuade ourselves, we are essentially on the side of time, while things, by contrast, inhabit the domain of space. But things also provide an indispensable adjunct to our sense of emergence and elapsing, duration and disappearance, forgetting and recall. Precisely because we feel ourselves to be made of time, we need the solidifying supplements of things to mark and grasp its passage. Things provide the relay through which we are able to tick time off, to bring it home to ourselves. Indeed, the passage of time is perhaps only really ascertainable by deduction from the degree of resistance put up by things; the longer and more stubbornly things hold out against it, the more sluggishly time will seem to pass; the more quickly they succumb to or are used up by time, the faster time seems to go. Things tell the time. Usually, they do this precisely by not staying in step with us – thus a 1990s mobile phone can seem more antique than a turn-of-the-century mangle.

So, if things give us our bearings in time, they can also, paradoxically, seem to suspend, syncopate, or otherwise snag time's steady unfolding. This is particularly the case during times of rapid material change like that experienced over the last two centuries. The particular things with which this book is concerned are most interesting when they are most interrupting: untimely, anachronistic. They are our counterparts and our companions, while never being exactly our contemporaries, for they can never quite get in step either with us or with themselves. This is why so many of the things we find most fascinating are those with which we have had a forgotten intimacy, and which suddenly come back to us after long separation – the madeleine cake which prompted Proust to the writing of *À la recherche du temps perdu*, the stinging sourness of a sherbet lemon tasted in Sydney, forty years and 12,000 miles away from my last one.

Precisely because they instance the once-new, things can impart the shock of the newly old. Such things inhabit space, but are a kind of temporising with it, a refracting of the white noon of the now into a chronic rainbow of times, with their twilight tints and hues. Such things hum with hint and import because they are there without being fully present; to hand, but not exactly *here-and-now*. Intimate and exotic, such things 'link us to our losses', in Philip Larkin's phrase.[3] They may be said to be our *haunts*; because they hang around us so, we are condemned and content, like unquiet ghosts, to frequent them. Untimely things like those on which I meditate in this book are unstopped clocks, miniature time bombs, that, going off at unpredictable times, can pull time itself apart.

Paraphernalia

This is why the question of the naming of things – often itself a magical operation – will often be important. As I began by saying, objects that exceed their simple being-there, whose being is a kind of exceeding, can also seem to exceed their naming, and so call for names to which some of this sense of the fuzzy or out-of-focus may cling. Indeed, thinking about the names of magical objects will often turn out to be part of their magical operation. In trying to think of a title for this book, I was looking for a common denominator for all these common-or-garden things that nevertheless seem to exceed their mere existence, or point beyond their primary function. What would be the name for a collection of such what's-its-names? What sort of thing in general might these generic things – these dangly, pointy, bendy, stretchy, sticky, shiny things – be said to be?

There was a range of candidate names, all of them what might be called disparate singulars. One of the generic names we employ for such things is simply 'stuff'. This word is interestingly two-sided. Though it can imply the valueless, that which is of little account – as in 'stuff and nonsense' – the word 'stuff' has actually come down in the world considerably, for it was often used in the medieval and Renaissance periods to refer to rare and costly fabrics. Nowadays, the point about stuff is that it is indeterminate, that it is a matter of indifference what specific kinds of matter it is made of. And yet 'stuff' can also signify deep personal attachment, as in the anguished cry of the traveller whose suitcase has been lost – 'but it had all my *stuff* in it!' We use the word 'stuff' as a verbal place-filler too, either when no other word comes to mind, or when no other word is available that has precisely the kind of imprecision that 'stuff' has.

There are more specialised words for particular kinds of stuff. For a while, I leant towards two of these for which I have a particular fondness: 'kit' and 'gear'. A 'kit' originally referred to a receptacle, such as a box or a basket, but then came to refer to the articles that it might contain, in particular the contents of a soldier's knapsack. This gave rise, first, to the oddly tautological expression 'kit-bag', a word which, meaning literally a bag-bag, or a bag for the contents of a bag, seems pleasingly to be full of itself, and then to the set of implements that might be required for a particular occupation, like that of a cobbler or burglar. The word was then in turn extended, in something of the same way as the word 'stuff', to refer to the whole of a collection of disparate things, as in the expressions 'the whole kit and boiling of them', 'the whole kit and cargo' and, still just about surviving, the marvellous, mysterious 'kit and caboodle', in which 'caboodle' is probably an alliterative improvement of 'boodle', which itself just means the whole lot of something. More recently, of course, 'kit' has come to mean clothing, as in sports kit, or, more generally, in the invitation to 'get your kit off'.

A similar word, though of more venerable lineage, is the word 'gear', which has been in use for centuries to refer to the equipment required for a particular purpose – as in riding gear, or an aircraft's landing gear. The word seems to derive from words meaning simply to make, or to make ready. It is related to the adjective 'yare', which meant fit for purpose, well-equipped or, if applied to a boat, trimly responsive to the rudder, and which mutated during the 1950s and 1960s into the hip adjectival usage 'gear', to mean good, attractive, or cool. Like 'kit', 'gear' has come to refer principally to clothing. It has in the past followed the word 'stuff' in referring to confused, formless or worthless nonsense. It has also on occasion been used to

mean pus, or other foul matter, and (like 'kit', too, actually) the genitals (but then there seem to be very few words that don't end up
referring to the genitals). I'd be prepared to risk the generalisation
that, as the use of any object becomes habitual, it starts to approach
the condition of something we wear, or have about our persons (a
habit is, after all, an item of clothing as well as a form of behaviour),
a kind of attire, on account of being drawn towards us (*ad-tirare*, to
pull towards).

In the end, though the things on which I meditate in what follows might very well have been rounded up under the rubrics of
Stuff, Kit or Gear, I have called them, collectively, Paraphernalia.
Unlike the other terms, this one has a Graeco-Latin rather than a
Germanic origin, and also has what at first sight may seem an
unhelpfully precise and restricted legal definition. In Roman law,
the *parapherna* were those items of property which were held by a
wife over and above the items in her dowry, these items remaining
her own; typically, this might be clothing, jewellery, and even furniture. In English and Scottish Common Law, in which, until the
Married Women's Property Act of 1870, a wife's property became
her husband's, her paraphernalia was a certain amount of personal
property which could be exempted from this condition and kept as
her own. The Latin word comes from the Greek *pherne*, a dowry,
formed from the word *pherein*, to bear or carry, as that which is
borne or carried into the marriage. The Latin *fer*, to carry, or bear,
changes in Germanic languages to *ber*, giving words like *bear*, and
their many derivatives. The association with women's personal
things means that 'paraphernalia' unfortunately connotes the incidental and the accessory, with a suggestion of the trivial. But the
word has also migrated to other contexts, being used to name the

particular kinds of apparatus or equipment used in the conduct of an occupation, such as medicine or law. Even in these specialised contexts, paraphernalia, like stuff, gear and clobber, retains the idea of a diffuse miscellany.

But the most important and expressive thing about this word is the prefix *para-*, which signifies something alongside but in addition, equivalent but extra. There is nothing essential about paraphernalia, which is why it has come to suggest unnecessary complication or elaboration, an exaggerated but ultimately empty exhibition of technical details. The word, which gives the impression of specifying some very precise kind of thing, like 'paraphilia', 'paranoia' or the 'paranormal', is in this respect self-instancing and self-performing, the word itself having a slightly meretricious ostentation that carries across to the things it names.

Like stuff, gear, kit and clobber, the essential thing about paraphernalia is that it is both unnecessary and yet for that very reason most needful to us. It is both *de trop* and indispensable. When you are really on the breadline what matters most are not the necessities that are meant to monopolise your thoughts, but the tiny treats or luxuries that you do not really need. As King Lear protests, when his daughters try to persuade him that he does not need to bring his entire retinue with him when he visits them, 'O! reason not the need; our basest beggars /Are in the poorest thing superfluous / Allow not nature more than nature needs, / Man's life is cheap as beast's'.[4] The only thing that is truly essential is the excessive. What prevents us relapsing into a purely animal or mechanical existence are precisely those unnecessary things that are the tiny, persisting proof of our existence, by which I mean our defining unnecessariness, the fact that there is no particular need for us to have arisen at all. To exist in this way is to be necessarily accidental, and the things to which I have tried to find ways of paying attention in this book are our necessary accessories in that.

Paraphernalia also joins together the impersonal and the personal. The paraphernalia of a particular occupation includes all the things that one would expect of any follower of that occupation, whether window cleaner or High Court judge – ladders, buckets, wigs, hammers and gavels. But our personal paraphernalia is also what we need for the occupation of being ourselves. As our fund of necessary accessories, that do not have to be ours and yet somehow makes us what we are, our paraphernalia is both anonymous and intimate, arbitrary and intrinsic. It is the kind of stuff that is found, or, just as often, lost, in places like drawers, cupboards and pockets, which, though they often contain very similar and predictable kinds of object – keys, pins, pills, elastic bands – also constitute something like involuntary abstracts or personal archives, that bear our signatures, have our lives in their charge and may one day amount to what we were.

1

Bags

If you were to disembark on this earth from another planet, what would be the thing that would strike you most about humans, compared with other species? It would not, I think, be the possession of language, the capacity to laugh, or to remember, or to use tools, or any of these more tra-ditional prerogatives that human beings like to accord to themselves. It would be our need, apparently unshared by any other species, to carry things around with us. We are not *homo erectus*, or *homo sapiens*, but *homo ferens*. If we like retrievers and gun dogs, it is because we are like them in our tenderness about the act of carrying things.

In the Academy of Lagado, Swift's Lemuel Gulliver hears of a scheme to abolish words, on the principle that they are only the names for things, so that it would be better to carry around in a bag all the things that they may have occasion to refer to during the day, the only drawback with this scheme being that very eloquent persons might require a caravan of bearers to assist them in transporting all of the things to which they may wish to allude.[1] Human beings have evolved fantastic and still-expanding ways in which to avoid the necessity to carry the world around, language being the most important. Yet the need persists to bear the weight of things. I am a light traveller by preference; my heart droops at the thought of having to cram my possessions into bags that I will then have to lug around with me wherever I go. I look forward to the day when I can step off the aeroplane in shorts and trainers, have my security details scanned via subcutaneous bar code and walk straight out of the airport. We all tell ourselves at times that we would be better off less encumbered – if we had less 'emotional baggage', for example. And yet, like everybody else, I also find travelling without luggage intolerable. It is not the emotions that are the baggage, it is baggage that stirs and secretes emotion. We are beings apt to feel unbearably light without 'our things'. We don't seem to be able to transport ourselves without transporting things with us. Bags mean this possibility. Bags mean ownership, identity, self-possession. They are memory, the weight of all we have been. 'Bags I!' children used to say; 'that's not my bag, man', as jazzmen and hippies had it.

Human beings are given to conceiving of themselves in terms of bags and receptacles. The mother's breast is perhaps at the origin of the sense of promise and secret goodness attaching to bags, and embodied in Santa's bulging sack. Our stories are full of the excitement of delicious and dangerous powers hidden away in bags; letting the cat out of the bag is a dangerous and exciting proceeding, as was Ulysses' release of the winds from the bag of Aeolus, the wind god. Sausages and saveloys were sometimes known in the nineteenth century as 'bags of mystery'.[2]

Because they are in essence such fleshly or bodily things, bags enact as nothing else does our sense of the relation between inside and outside. We are creatures who find it easy and pleasurable to imagine living on the inside of another body; we ourselves come into independent existence very slowly, being carried, like bags, for long enough to come to know this intermediate condition intimately, and never to be able to forget it. Human beings make the world into bags, because holding things together, holding things up, and being ourselves held and held up, are so important to us. Infant humans are carried for longer than any other creature. 'Independence' literally means 'not hanging'. For no other creature, it seems, are carrying and being carried so inextricably a part of one's identity. This is indicated clearly enough in the many different senses in which carrying and carriage are threaded through our language. Carrying things is important for how we carry ourselves. The fact that we understand so well what it is to be carried, what it is to be in a bag, or to be like one, accounts for our concern for and even tenderness towards bags. We carry bags, but we design them also to cling on to us, our shoulders, or the crooks of our arms, or even to hang at our waists. When we give bags handles, we give them hands. Bags are the little people we once were and still are. We love portable property because that's how we began. Since the months in which I carried my babies in slings, I have been unable to see or hold a bag without tenderness. Bags must be treated with care because of the life there is in them. It is difficult to be wholly without grace when carrying a bag.

Lives are full of bags. Bags are full of lives.

Bags join space to time. We do indeed, in every sense, 'bear children'. Both 'bearing' and 'carrying' conjoin the meanings of holding up and holding out: of supporting, holding and transporting through space, and enduring or lasting out through time. You bear an ordeal, or carry out a task, or hold on through suffering, as though time were something experienced as a kind of weight. 'Time', we say, 'hangs heavy'. To bear, to carry, means to endure, to last out; to carry and to carry on, to carry over, to endure: weight means time: so weight means waiting. Samuel Beckett puns lengthily on the two different kinds of wait in his play *Waiting for Godot*, which contains a memorable bag-carrier in the person of Lucky, the slave of the tyrant Pozzo, who spends most of the play encumbered by his master's enormous bags. Because he is kept at the end of a long rope tied around his neck, Lucky is himself a kind of bag, more or less. Estragon, one of the two tramps who meet Pozzo and Lucky in the indeterminate landscape of the play, is tormented by the question 'Why doesn't he put down his bags?', asking it again and again.[3] The question itself holds up the action, which in this play of ultimate inaction, actually means keeping it going. When eventually Lucky does put down his bags, in order to start incomprehensibly thinking out loud, the others find his monologue intolerable, and beat him to the ground. Carrying not only weighs us down, it also, it appears, keeps us up.

In fact, Samuel Beckett is probably the great, hitherto uncelebrated dramatist of bags. In his play *Happy Days*, the first act of which is the monologue of a woman buried up to her waist in a mound of earth, the action is punctuated and parcelled out by Winnie's plunges and sallies into her bag for lipstick, toothpaste, mirror, medicine, and all the possibilities they embody of beguiling the vicious time of her existence – 'Perhaps just one quick dip', she says, as a boozer to his tipple.[4] When, in the second act, she is inhumed up to her neck, the horror of her situation is signalled most of all by the bag which lies on the mound, tauntingly gaping just in sight and to hand, though for the handless Winnie now unreachable, as though all the resources of life and memory and history were held inaccessibly in it.

Bags are female-seeming objects, and have strong associations with female experience in many cultures. Few women are able to bear the horror of male fingers rummaging in their handbags, and surely there is no man who has not at some time itched to do this. In Britain and America, subtle, untaught but unbreachable rules still govern the kind of bags that men and women can feel comfortable holding or carrying. One of the rules seems to be that the floppier the bag, the less male it seems. More bizarre still is the implicit ordinance concerning the length of the handle. The longer the handles of a bag, the more effeminate the bag, perhaps because the more handle there is attached to a bag, the more it can appear to be something hanging on to you, rather than something that you are actively holding. And then, for reasons which I cannot easily explain, a man's masculinity seems more compromised by a string bag than any other kind. But then why do women, whom men delight in imagining to be made up almost entirely of dark recesses and hidden cavities, usually have no pockets? My father used to say that somebody or something was 'as useless as a pocket in a singlet'. But such a thing has only to be named for me to be able to imagine its marsupial comfort and utility. I would willingly wear a singlet in secret, something I have never done, if only to have the knowledge of such a thing about my person.

In every household I know, there is a special place where plastic carrier bags are hoarded. A drawer, or a box, or, nine times out of ten, a bag of bags. What is it for? What is the meaning of this? Perhaps because there is always something ruthless or insulting about simply throwing away a bag. In our cellar, we have an even more marvellous contrivance. It is a luggage nest. On the outside, there is a large, firm, capacious suitcase, snapped shut with latches. Inside that, there is a slightly smaller suitcase; unzip that, and there is an aptly named holdall, clasped tightly round a vanity case, and then a series of ever tinier, more tightly budded pouches, purses and pods. And round the outside, holding together the whole bulging, intestinal contraption, there is a sheet of polythene against the dust, swollen skintight. It is a body we have got down there, a cannibal organism that binges on and breeds itself. I have just remembered that, when I was at school, the girls used to bring in anatomical dolls, that you could fold open to reveal their inner organs. Kneeling in front of our luggage nest, my hand plunging through the layers, groping for the little overnight bag that is several layers in, I am performing the same play-Caesareans as they used to in the playground.

If bags irresistibly suggest wombs, bellies and breasts, and may suggest an identification with women in their containing function, they have some distinctively male features, too. For the shape of bags is periodic, bags being defined by a rhythm of alternation between rigidity and collapse. Held, or worn, or carried, bags come into their own, assume and hold their own shapes. Put down, bags sag and crumple, their rigidity and definition ebbing from them. And bags offer quickening excitement in the contrast between hard and soft shapes: the pillowcase on Christmas morning, jutting with exciting knobs, elbows and corners, or the inverse, the impermeable outer casing containing folded softness.

You can think of bags as concrete meditations on the nature of human weight and shape. The principle of a bag is that it runs from the skimpiest form, which does nothing but wrap its contents, through to the sturdiest skeleton, which gives no clue as to the size or shape or weight of what lies inside. It is the operative difference between women, who cannot give birth without having to change their shapes, and men, who may think of themselves as impermeable and undentable, but who nevertheless know, perhaps even more intimately than women, the bag-like rhythm of tumescence and collapse. Bag makers and bag users relish the jokes this contrast allows: a lock on a floppy bag is the most lovely and skilful silliness imaginable.

How we carry bags is important. Bags are carried in the hand, in the crook of the arm, over the shoulder, on the back. In the form of pockets, bags can bloat and blister out on chests, thighs and hips. Our liking for the bodily supplements of baggage extends to our means of transport, which have bags attached to them, from saddlebags to the boots of coaches and cars. The bellies of aircraft bulge with our bags. About ten years ago, I remember, girls took to wearing tiny, exquisitely functionless little rucksacks, like a bulging third eye or a ganglion in the middle of their backs. It was as though they had a little growing homunculus clinging to them. Bags are our most intimate daimons, even when we wear them most casually strung around our necks or on our backs.

Just as we sleep in sleeping bags, we have a need to restore ourselves to bags and sacks when we die, just as we come from bags and sacks in getting born. This is why we find the idea of putting a body straight into the ground so difficult to live with, and why bags and sacks are associated with death just as much as they are with life.

Nineteenth-century resurrectionists, who dug up newly buried bodies for the purposes of medical dissection, were known as 'sack 'em up men'. The closer we are to death, the more like bags we become, the more we sag and dangle, the more we are weighed down with rather than carrying ourselves. War means servicemen coming home in body bags. The First World War poet Isaac Rosenberg refers to the body of a soldier reduced vilely to mere matter as the 'soul's sack'.[5]

So, as well as goodness and wealth and plump promise, bags are also the sign of indigence and indignity, uselessness and superannuation. To give somebody the sack derives from the phrase, common in the eighteenth and nineteenth centuries, 'to give someone the bag to hold'. A woman who left a man at a dance to flirt with another would give him the metaphorical bag to hold, the idea being, I suppose, that to be left holding somebody's bag, uselessly hanging on, or hanging around, is to be reduced to the condition of a bag. Holding the bag, the jiltee would have become the bag, in the same way that being given the sack is to be made as useless as one. And yet, there is no beggar so poor as to be unaccommodated with a bag of some kind; in the late sixteenth century, to 'turn to bag and wallet' meant to become a beggar.[6] Tramps and bag ladies need bags for their self-possession, to make the nothing they have, and are considered to be, into a kind of portable property.

Bags also have a sonorous dimension, nowhere more unmistakably than in the bagpipe, the very image of the pseudo-life of the body as simply a bag of winds, a lung, or belly, or scrotum, and nothing more. The history of music is full of repeated stand-offs between stringed and wind instruments (the prime example being the myth of the contest between Apollo and Marsyas) and the low status of wind instruments accounts in part for the association which grew in medieval Europe between bagpipes and fools.[7] The bauble, or bladder on a stick with which jesters were traditionally provided seems to be linked to their function as emitters of nonsensical vacancy, or hot air; the 'bauble' or 'bayble' carried by the fool was sometimes a head on a stick, sometimes a bladder full of air. The word 'bladder' derives from Old Teutonic *blaê-drôn*, from a verb stem *blaê*, to blow, and *drôn*, contrivance or instrument, and this word spawns a number of words for noisy, vacuous, windbag speech, of the kind that one might imagine would issue from a bladder, like 'blether' and 'blither'.

Bags are antique and ageing things. You can call someone an old bag, but it would be ridiculous to call someone a young bag. We carry more and more bags about our persons, which themselves become more and more bag-like, as we age. Clothes enact our relationship to this ageing into the state of bags, rags, luggage, stuff. Our very clothes keep us clear of death and age only as long as they hold us, the function of clothes not at all being to cover, but to contain and sustain. Is there a grimmer witness to our good riddance than our clothes when they are emptied of us – a tossed sock, or a tangled brassiere? The absurd futility of baggage at the approach of death identifies baggage with death's ultimate beggary. Perhaps this is why packing, even in the midst of life, is always a bit like picking over and putting away the possessions of the newly dead.

2

Batteries

 **Of all depleted or superseded things**, the hardest for me to dispose of are batteries. The kind of battery I have in mind here is the ordinary domestic kind which is used to power familiar items like torches, doorbells, razors and radios, as opposed to, say, industrial or car batteries. Though batteries come in all shapes and sizes, the ideal form of the battery, and not, I think, just because it is the most commonly used, is what is known as the AA battery. AA batteries sit snugly in the palm or the fist, and yet, held by their ends, pleasingly push apart and span the thumb and second finger. Hold these two fingers up now, as though you were holding an AA battery, and I think you will find that you can estimate its size to within a millimetre. Although I must acknowledge the charms of the many forms of square and rectangular battery with which I am also on terms, and which tend to be marketed as 'power packs', they always seem cruder and more

rough-hewn to me than their sophisticated city-slicker cousins, the cylinder batteries. Open up the bonnet of a car and, no matter how sleek and gleaming the array of pipes, devices and instruments may be, the square battery will always seem like a raw and archaic thing. A battery that squats on its base as a box-type battery does may suggest a chunky kind of four-square self-evidence, but the capacity of a cylinder battery both to stand slimly upright and to skate away with such surprising speed across anything but the most perfectly flat surface (an AA battery doubles excellently as a spirit level) makes it an altogether more perverse and versatile kind of object.

We get through dozens of these batteries in our household, but, if I find it hard to throw them away, it is hardly at all, if I am honest, for environmental reasons. It is that, when I slide my thumb over their unscarred, slightly glutinous lustre, and hear that dry clank of theirs when I drop them into a bin, I can only abstractly persuade myself that they are no longer of use. This is irritating for all concerned, since, unlike cartons of milk, which, once drained of their contents, are reduced to flimsy husks, or spent light bulbs, which, when shaken, may emit the telltale little salt-sift of their broken filaments, or even used matches which so many people feel the reverent instinct to return to their box, batteries remain the same in their discharged condition, cool, smooth, glossy, as when they were in their pack, serenely brimful of their humming promise. They suffer no discernible diminution of weight or mass. They do not usually corrode or scuff or peel. These darling buds give without giving out, without having to devolve their tightly folded forms into blossom and ragged rot, which means that duds or has-beens are identical to primed batteries. The exception to this is when you open the battery compartments of appliances you have not used for some time to discover the batteries coated with a horrifyingly squamous crust of decomposition.

One of the most delightful things about batteries is that their power can be increased by simple accumulation, in a way that seems both intuitively and childishly right. Yes, four batteries strapped together actually do produce four times the power of one, just as two potatoes take twice as long to microwave as one does. The clusters in which batteries are arranged in the snug alcoves provided for them in cameras and torches make me think of the six-packs of dynamite sticks, taped together at the waist, and with a fizzing fuse issuing from their midst, that are always miraculously available for cartoon characters when faced with some intractable obstacle. A car battery is known as an accumulator, and batteries do indeed offer reassuring proof of the more-is-more logic of elementary accumulation (the more flies you eat, the thinner you are supposed to get).

Curiously, given the fiddling, inquisitive kind of child I was, especially when it came to electrical apparatus, the inner anatomy of a battery has never held much allure for me. This is only partly because of the difficulty of breaking open its top or filing through its metal casing to inspect its innards. I was, and am, intellectually curious about what exists and occurs inside a battery, but I feel obscurely enjoined to leave it in obscurity, knowing that somehow whatever I found inside would be bound to fall short of the delicious half-knowledge I feel I have about it. In fact, a battery has the mystical self-sufficiency of a stone, the composure that comes from seeming to have no inside, and being the same all the way through. This makes me appreciative of the instinct of people like Wun Chok Bong, who interprets menhirs and standing stones as generators, conductors and reservoirs of force. Bong's argument is that megalithic monuments are in fact stores of energy – 'dry cell batteries of the Gods' – used by intergalactic visitors to the Earth in the same way as the supply dumps set up by mountaineers.[1] The artist Joseph Beuys made a number of works which drew on and indulged the widespread willingness to believe that the simple material differences between things might be the source of a kind of energy. One of these is *Fat Battery* (1963), a box with various objects in fat and felt which are intended to resemble the components of a battery. One of the last works he made was *Capri Battery* (1985), which consists of a light bulb plugged into a lemon, with a note reading 'Charge the battery after a thousand hours'. This keeps alive an ancient way of thinking of the physical world as a complex arena of affinities and antagonisms, of stores and drains of energy.

But the most important part of the implicit magic of a battery is that it can be seen as a kind of animate body. So mysterious has the electrical force seemed from its very beginnings that animate powers have often been attributed to it. In fact, the invention of the battery has a direct relation to the idea of human or animal electricity. In 1771, the Italian physiologist Luigi Galvani noticed that an electrical charge accidentally discharging to earth through a dead frog's leg produced a convulsive twitch. This led him to suggest that the frog's body was a kind of reservoir of positive and negative electrical charge. What we would now call the electrical potential between the differently charged nerve and muscle tissue of the frog made it in effect a battery.[2]

Experiments and speculations about electricity through the eighteenth century gave Galvani good warrant to think as he did. For one thing, the electricity that was known about was the same as that noticed in ancient Greece when amber (Greek *electron*) was rubbed, namely, static electricity. The governing theory that electricity (like heat) was a kind of superfine substance, rather than a force (the flow of electrons), must have encouraged the kind of thinking that saw electricity as something to be accumulated and then discharged. In 1746, the invention of the Leyden jar made it possible to store large amounts of electric potential, which in its turn encouraged experiments with and demonstrations of electrical healing.[3] The Leyden jar consisted of a vessel full of water, with tinfoil wrapped around the inside and outside, into which a metal conductor was dipped. When static electricity was generated by friction, the conducting wire transmitted through the water a positive charge to the inside surface of the tinfoil. When a human subject gripped the conducting wire and the outside tinfoil, a circuit was created, and a strong electric shock ensued.

There was a great deal of showmanship in the investigation of electricity, and most of it involved exhibiting its effects on the human body. There was great excitement about the capacity of the human body both to store and to conduct electricity. Perhaps the first human battery was displayed by Stephen Gray in 1730. He suspended an eight-year-old boy from a silk rope and gave him an electrostatic charge by applying to his feet a glass tube charged by friction. The boy was then able to attract to himself brass leaf and other light objects.[4] An even more impressive display was the 'apotheosis' or 'beatification' developed by Georg Mathias Bose, in which a man seated on a chair suspended from silk threads or, later on, on a large slab of insulating pitch was similarly charged.[5] His charge partly ionised the air around him, so that, with the lights off, 'by little and little a lambent Flame arises from the Pitch, and spreads itself around his Feet; from hence by Degrees it is propagated to his Knees, his Body, and at last to his Head ... by continuing the Electrisation the Man's Head is surrounded by a Glory, such a one in some measure, as is represented by Painters in their ornamenting the Heads of Saints'.[6]

Displays like this, along with excited speculation that electricity might be the mysterious vital force that joined soul and body, made it easy to see human bodies as condensers of electrical fluid. Galvani's view of the frog as possessed of a special, indwelling kind of animal electricity might also have been encouraged by the extensive eighteenth-century interest in the torpedo and the electric eel, both of which seemed to prove beyond dispute that, at least in principle, animals could be possessed of electrical potential.[7]

However, Galvani soon found an opponent in Alessandro Volta, who had discovered that the contact of dissimilar metals was enough on its own to generate an electrical charge. Volta argued that the frog's muscle twitched because an external electrical current was passing through it, rather than because of any intrinsic electrical force. For some years, between 1791, the year in which Galvani announced the frog's convulsion to the world, and 1800, arguments spat and crackled as to whether the frog was the source or merely the vehicle of the electrical energy. Finally, Volta invented a device that seemed to make it plain that electricity was indeed generated by the contact of different materials. The Voltaic battery, or 'pile' (the name that is still used in French), was simply that, a column of alternating silver and zinc discs, separated by wads of paper soaked in brine.[8]

It used to be thought that the only kind of electricity known before Volta was the electrostatic electricity that was gathered in the Leyden jar. In fact, around 1936, a vase dating from around 2000 years ago was discovered in Iraq that gives every appearance of having functioned as a Voltaic battery, containing as it did a copper tube inside which was inserted an iron needle.[9] With the addition of some easily available acid such as lemon juice or vinegar, it could certainly have generated an electric charge, though it is not clear what its purpose was. Electroplating has been suggested, as has, more recently and, I think, more probably, some kind of therapeutic use.[10]

Volta proclaimed his invention as the end of the debate with Galvani and the final seeing off of the idea of animal electricity. Oddly enough, though, Volta himself muddied the issue with references to the endogenous electrical energy of the torpedo fish, which he called a *natural electric organ*, in contrast to the *artificial electric organ* of his devising. Indeed, he says explicitly that his apparatus is 'much more similar in its fundamentals, as I will make clear, and even in the way I have constructed it, to the *natural electric organ* of the torpedo, the electric eel, etc, than to the Leyden bottle and the electric batteries that we know'. He even suggests sealing the column and joining the discs, by which means, 'the discs would be a fairly good imitation of an electric eel'. The resemblance could be made even stronger, he suggests, 'if the discs could be joined together by pliable metal wires or screw springs, and its entire length covered in skin and with a well-made head and tail at its extremities'.[11] Volta is thinking principally about the sensational appearance such an apparatus might make in the kind of 'shocks and sparks' electrical exhibition that had been common for half a century.[12] Even though he claims that the distinctive feature of his apparatus is that it possesses 'an inexhaustible charge, a perpetual action or impulse on the electrical fluid',[13] he seems much more concerned with the nature of the sensations that the electric current imparts, to hands, fingers, tongue, ears and even, strewth, eyes, than with its potential uses. Indeed, it is difficult for us to appreciate how almost entirely and gloriously gratuitous Volta's marvellous invention was, before any of the thousands of portable devices that would make use of it had been conceived.[14] Ironically, given that Volta is regularly regarded as having grasped the truth of electricity because he was a physicist rather than a physiologist, the uses he imagines for electricity seem principally to have been medical.[15] Volta's battery was in fact what batteries remain, a kind of magic for the body, that is itself a kind of magic body.

The principal use of the battery during the first decades of its existence was not to provide a continuous flow of power. Rather it was to make it convenient to deliver sudden jolts of electricity, in a movement that often discharged the battery all at once. The battery remains closely associated with the idea of the spark, an energy that leaps suddenly across intervening space, and the cooperating notion of what might be called the charged gap. Contradicting the tendency for things gradually to merge, mingle and blur, the vital spark is sudden, convulsive, catastrophic, absolute, exhausting and animating at once, redemptive. Who among us now can read the extended finger of the Lord reaching out to Adam in Michelangelo's *Creation* as anything other than the terminal of a deific battery about to transmit the spark of life?

Volta's invention did little to dispel, and did plenty to encourage, the magical idea of vital electricity. The most powerful enthusiast for Volta's work was Napoleon Bonaparte, who was ravished by a demonstration of the battery in Paris in November 1801. He seems spectacularly but tellingly to have missed the point of what Volta had achieved, when he turned to his physician Corvisart during the demonstration and exclaimed 'Here, my good doctor, we have the image of life itself! The pile represents the column of vertebrae, the liver is the negative pole, the kidneys, the positive pole!'[16]

Thus, despite having apparently comprehensively lost the argument, Galvani's ideas took root in traditions of magical thinking. In the mid-nineteenth century a popular scientific writer called J. O. N. Rutter revived the idea of animal electricity, arguing for the reality of the 'frog-battery' of Galvani. Rutter was in fact what might be called a pan-electricist, in that he thought that 'all substances, animate and inanimate, contain electricity. It is, in the largest sense of the term, a universal agent'. But he was keen to convince his readers that 'the living organism is a source of electricity' and that the human body in particular was a generator of energy.[17] His book has a frontispiece showing a woman with her hands in two bowls of water, observing the current registered by an attached apparatus Rutter calls the 'galvanoscope'. In the same year, Benjamin Brodie compared the generation of 'nervous force' by the action of oxygenised blood on the brain to 'the action of the acid solution on the metallic plates in the cells of a voltaic battery'.[18] The battery was a central agent in the revival of therapeutic electricity that took place in the nineteenth century.[19] 'Body Batteries' became a staple of quack electrotherapy in the 1880s and 1890s. They often took the form of some kind of truss or body belt, such as 'C.N. West's Electro Medical Belt', designed to tone and vitalise its users, which promised unreassuringly that 'its electricity is so *mild* that a *babe* can wear it, yet so *strong* that it will pass through a *No. 17* Copper wire, 10,000 miles in length, and *cauterise the skin*'.[20]

Not surprisingly, the occult and magical traditions also seized on the metaphor of the battery. The inventor of theosophy, Madame Blavatsky, referred to the 'soul-electricity' generated by 'the cerebral pile' of man.[21] The theosophist Anna Kingsford explained that the large number of spiritual adepts originating from the Orient was because 'the soil and astral fluid there are charged with power as a vast battery of many piles. So that the Hierarch of the Orient both is himself an older soul and has the magnetic support of a chain of older souls, and the earth beneath his feet and the medium around him are charged with electric force in a degree not to be found elsewhere'.[22] Writing as 'Yogi Ramacharaka', William Atkinson promised that 'We may store away prana [the life-force in the air we breathe], just as the storage battery stores away electricity'.[23] Writing under a different pen name, that of 'Magus Incognito', Atkinson gets even more symbolic output from the idea of the battery in his *Secret Doctrine of the Rosicrucians*, from which we learn that:

> From the 'cathode' pole of the battery emerge the great swarms of electrons, ions, or corpuscles; and from the same pole also emerge the wonderful 'rays' which have played such an important part in modern physics. The 'cathode' pole of the battery is the Mother of all that strange brood of new forms of matter which have appeared to confute the old materialistic theories, and to destroy the old conceptions of science. The 'cathode' pole should, in reality and truth, be called the 'female' pole; and the 'positive' the 'male,' for such terms truly represent their true respective offices.[24]

An early twentieth-century popular introduction to Zen Buddhism promised that meditation or 'dhyâna' could be regarded as 'physiologically the accumulation of nervous energy; it is a sort of spiritual storage battery in which an enormous amount of latent force is sealed, – a force which will, whenever demand is made, manifest itself with tremendous potency'.[25] The writer Upton Sinclair declared in 1930 that '[t]he human brain is a storage battery, capable of sending impulses over the nerves', and wondered 'Why may it not be capable of sending impulses by means of some other medium, known or unknown? Why may there not be such a thing as brain radio?'[26] Just as the battery appears like a magical embodiment of the idea of a storable force, so dreams of exercising this force borrow from the material form of the battery.

The fantasy of the human battery found an embodiment in my early life in the children's puppet TV series *Torchy the Battery Boy*, which was first aired on British TV in 1958. At the beginning of the series, a lonely old toymaker laments 'I wish I had a little boy of my own, who would help me. Oh! I've a wonderful idea! I'll make a toy boy! Now then, how can I make a toy who can walk, and talk, and do all the things that real boys do? Now let me see. I've got it! I'll put a torch battery inside him, and when I press the switch, he'll come to life!' The scene of Torchy's animation is a cross between *Pinocchio* and *Frankenstein*; Torchy himself had the fixed, wide-eyed stare and the slightly inebriated squawk of the ventriloquist's dummy, while the magic beam of the cyclopean lamp mounted in his head has x-ray and telephonic powers and can locate lost objects. A darker application of the human-battery idea was provided by *The Matrix* (1999), which, running together the ideas of battery hens and electrical batteries, imagines millions of human beings suspended in liquid in order to supply bio-electricity for a future robot civilisation.

In one sense, batteries seem anachronistic in a networked world in which part of us feels that everything ought to be available on tap, wherever and whenever we want it. This was very much how things seemed at the end of the nineteenth century, when the principal use for the battery was to provide back-up and load equalisation for power stations. Some dreamed of harvesting power from lightning, or the 'storage battery of the air'.[27] Nikola Tesla, the inventor of alternating current, had a visionary plan for radio towers that would broadcast electrical power. It was the streetcar, with its complex, changeable needs, and, following this, the automobile, which also needed onboard power, that led to the modern proliferation of batteries as the very form of portable power.[28]

Batteries are the magical embodiment of what may be called the principle of *charge*. This is the idea that energy is a kind of substance, which can be packed into a confined space. Batteries are potent because they are full of potential. Like many magical objects, they do not exist to fulfil a particular, designated purpose. A garden trowel or a toilet plunger can both of course be turned to different purposes, and there is a particular pleasure that comes from that. Members of the S & M community take giggly pleasure in the idea of what are called 'pervertibles', perfectly ordinary domestic implements, like clothes pegs, washing lines and, well, toilet plungers, I suppose, that may be turned to the subtle pleasures of unpleasantness. But trowels and toilet plungers seem nevertheless to have strongly specific affordance, bodying forth their official purposes in every aspect of their form. But where such objects are like skin cells or liver cells, batteries are pluripotent stem cells – things that exist to give other things power, to make other things possible. And yet, just for this reason, they are the signs of their own potential, they are the embodiment of the general possibility they embody, that is, the unlikely and unlooked-for possibility that possibility itself, that immaterial thing, could take on a physical form.

3

Buttons

 **I can think of no object** in common use that is more cross-temporally old-new than the button. Learning to button and unbutton oneself is a skill that, like tying a lace or a tie, we have all somehow, though too long ago to remember, acquired, a skill that is easy to perform but notoriously hard to describe or instruct a novice in. I can't remember ever being taught to sew on a button, either, though it has also been a rare occurrence for anyone ever to have done this for me. Like pins, buttons are fiddly things, with which it is hard not to fidget. The worship of sleekness and functionality in the 1960s made it obvious to makers of science fiction films and TV series in the period that buttons must be on their way out. The stripped-down, straight-up, streamlined future would have no time for all this fiddle-faddle, so its sheer all-in-one suits would be secured by zips and velcro (which would fasten diagonally, slashing

diagonality being the infallible sign of futurity's intolerance of fussy delay). As though in reaction to that factitious futurity, buttons started to reappear during the 1990s, for example in the button-fly of Levi jeans, as the sign of no-nonsense honesty and downhome straightforwardness.[1]

We had a tin in the house where I grew up for assorted buttons (the very word 'assorted', applied as it was in those days to so many things, including sweets and biscuits, summons up that era of mixtures and approximate associations in which buttons were in their prime). There is no more powerfully synecdochic object than a button, which offers to let one reconstruct the garment from which it came, just as the Victorian palaeontologist Richard Owen was reputed to be able, or to think himself able, to reconstruct an entire dinosaur from a single fossil. Our button tin in Hawthorn Road, which doubtless had once held toffees or acid drops, contained an entire imaginary currency; there were extravagantly large, high-denomination flat discs, some of mother-of-pearl, that had once surely belonged to fancy items of evening wear or dressing gowns; middle-value buttons for coats and trousers; and the small change of shirt buttons. The extraordinary variety of shapes and textures was accompanied by strange, musty perfumes. The button tin would be raided periodically to provide capital for our small-time domestic gambling at Ludo and Strip Jack Naked. There were also exotic items of what seemed like foreign or antique currency, the testudi, groats and denarii of the button currency market, many of which scarcely seemed like buttons at all; outlandish pegs and plugs, Joseph Grimaldi pompom buttons, buttons wound in silk and other fabrics, barrels, enamelled plaques, butterfly buttons and bowtie buttons. What on earth could they be for? The remote chance that one day a lounge suit or ball gown with exactly corresponding buttons (only with one missing) would turn up? Buttons, like keys, are part of an economy of lost belongings, and glow glumly with the melancholy sense that the fate of things is not so much to fall apart as to come undone or get lost.

Like so many other intimate objects, buttons are bodily. The word 'button' may be related to 'bud', and the word 'button' was used in eastern parts of England in just this sense. The undesirable buddings in the flesh of pimples and pustules have long been known as buttons (spots are still 'boutons' in French). 'Buttons of Naples' was the mock-honorific seventeenth-century name for syphilitic buboes.[2] Cotgrave's 1611 French-English dictionary memorably defines a 'bouton de verolle' as '*a pockie botch; or a high, and eminent pimple, bursting out in any part of a bodie infected with the pockes*'.[3] Sheep dung was also known as 'buttons' in Devon and the expression 'his tail makes buttons' was an expression transferred to humans to indicate the outward and visible signs of a state of terror and apprehension.[4] Silver breast-shaped buttons, with a nipple in the centre, were produced, mostly in Holland and Norway, during the eighteenth and nineteenth centuries.[5]

And, of course, the node of flesh where the foetus buds off from its mother will come to be known, once tied off, as its 'belly button'. Parents, in my day, and for all I know still in this, used to tell children that their belly buttons were there to hold their bottoms on. This information was less reassuring than I assume it was meant to be, though both 'button' and 'buttock' obligingly derive from Latin *bottare*, to push out or protrude. There are superstitions that suggest that the belly button really is thought of as a human being's hub or heart. I learn from the Heritage Coach Company blog (devoted to 'the discussion of all things related to funeral cars and limousines') that '[i]t is believed that grabbing a button on your clothing when passing hearses or funeral cars will help you stay "connected" to life and the living rather than death'.[6] There is a Japanese superstition that, if you sleep with your belly button exposed on a thundery night, you may wake up to find it has been stolen by the thunder god (to do what with, exactly? to eat? croon over? make new babies from?).[7]

The navel is certainly a numinous thing. To determine the *omphalos*, or centre of the earth, Jupiter sent two eagles flying in contrary directions, finding that they crossed at the oracle of Delphi. But the navel is also a permanent reminder that we did not and could not ever have given rise to ourselves, and that, like the buttons in the button tin, we are add-ons, afterthoughts, offcuts, branchings, sprouts. Like the button itself, which is only any good as long as there is a buttonhole to answer to it, we are sundered from our other halves, detached from our first attachments, ever at one remove from entirety.

Yet to get something 'on the button' is to get it right on target, an expression probably deriving from boxing, in which the button is the chin, though also looking back to the 'butt' that was the target in medieval archery. But (there is always a but with the button), if buttons have an identifying function, and seem to suffice to pin down things in themselves, they are also detachable, circulable and substitutable, and therefore vicarious, or place-holding, objects. They are therefore among the large class of things that function as 'quasi-objects', in Michel Serres' phrase, distributors or illuminators of subjectivity, ways of transferring or putting into circulation the quality of being 'it' in games.[8] In the game of 'Buttony', boys and girls stand in a line with closed eyes and hands held out, one of them receiving a button from a child known as 'Buttony' who goes along the line. 'Buttony' then challenges the children to guess who the recipient of the button has been and, if they guess correctly, the recipient takes the place of Buttony.[9]

The German word for button is *Knopf*, close to the English 'knob', another form of suggestive bodily protruberance. The buttonhole that accommodates the button's knob or bud has sometimes been identified with the vagina, and a 'buttonhole factory', in consequence, as a brothel, while a 'buttonhole-maker' was American slang for the parent exclusively of daughters.[10] Buttons are also implicated in other kinds of copulation between persons, most notably in the extraordinary practice that survives in the expression 'buttonholing', to mean securing somebody for conversation, in which one's interlocutor would literally hold one by the button, or hook a finger in a spare buttonhole for the space of the exchange – or rather, as often as not, the merciless monologue of the buttonholer. The fact that the original term for this was 'buttonholding' suggests that it was first of all the button of one's helpless auditor that was held and then subsequently a spare buttonhole. The most famous escape from this discursive predicament was that of Charles Lamb from his loquacious schoolmate Samuel Taylor Coleridge, here in Lamb's somewhat fanciful reconstruction:

> brimful of some new idea, and in spite of my assuring him that time was precious, he drew me within the door of an unoccupied garden by the roadside, and there, sheltered from observation by a hedge of evergreens, he took me by the button of my coat, and closing his eyes commenced an eloquent discourse, waving his right hand gently, as the musical words

flowed in an unbroken stream from his lips. I listened entranced; but the striking of a church-clock recalled me to a sense of duty. I saw it was of no use to attempt to break away, so taking advantage of his absorption in his subject, I, with my penknife, quietly severed the button from my coat, and decamped. Five hours afterwards, in passing the same garden, on my way home, I heard Coleridge's voice, and on looking in, there he was, with closed eyes – the button in his fingers – and his right hand gracefully waving, just as when I left him. He had never missed me![11]

Like many another everyday object, the button is a thing to fidget with, which is to say that it is a mediator of meditation – at once a distraction, and yet also the vehicle of the effort of our thinking to settle on, settle into, some material form. The button can be rocked, rotated, twisted, flicked, tilted, tugged, inverted. Fidgeting and fumbling with buttons surely recalls our very first plaything, with which every infant human first learns the arts of toying and temporising, the nipple.

Buttons splice us together with ourselves, halving us to make us one. Being buttoned up or buttoned down offers more reassurance, a greater sense of safety and self-coinciding, than any other kind of fastening. One need think only of the intolerable, unspeakable sense of unease attaching to the idea of being buttoned up wrongly of leaving a top or bottom button pitifully or ludicrously orphaned. To 'have a full set of buttons' is to be fully *compos mentis*, whereas to 'have a button missing' is to be daft or crazy. The buttons on a new waistcoat allowed for divination, by a counting rhyme such as 'sowja, salor, tinker, tailor, gentleman, apothecary, plow-boy, thief', or, in an alternative version from Arbroath, 'A laird, a lord, / A rich man, a thief, / A tailor, a drummer, / A stealer o' beef', told out down one's buttons, with one's destined condition predicted by whatever corresponded to the bottom button.[12]

One of the delightful sophistications of buttons is that they not only require buttonholes to complete their action, they also themselves incorporate holes, whether in the form of shanks attached to their reverse sides, or in holes drilled through them. Finding a button is thought to be lucky, but only if it has four holes rather than two.[13] But there is also such a thing as a single-holed button, known suggestively as a 'Bachelor Button' (also the name of a flower).

Buttons are a cipher for near-worthlessness – indeed, it became a word for a counterfeit coin, or, in a related usage, a decoy or sham buyer at an auction.[14] But buttons are also the emblems of standing and grandeur. In 1530, the artist Benvenuto Cellini, one of the greatest goldsmiths of his age, made a button for Pope Clement VII, which was mounted on gold and surrounded by diamonds, depicting God the Father surrounded by cherubs.[15] Such exorbitance in buttons has long been a sign of magnificence. Elizabeth I had a craving for buttons, and Louis XIV once handed over £22,000 for a set of six buttons.[16] Buttons seem to have been decorative rather than utilitarian until relatively recent times. Yet no buttons have been found in excavations of Greek sites. The reason usually given for this is suggestive of the boom-and-bust variability of the button's value; it is because they were either made of valuable materials that were recycled, or of negligable and perishable materials like wood which have decomposed. Some illustrations of Roman tunics have shoulder fastenings suggestive of buttons, but it is unlikely that they involved the sewn eyeholes that became common later.[17]

Buttons began to replace the fibula, the brooch or pin, by the early Middle Ages.[18] They were particularly useful for the tight fitting dress of the thirteenth century where they were often used in sleeves to close fabric from the wrist to the elbow, though during this period they still seem to have been more decorative than functional. As a result, they became the target of clerical censure and sumptuary regulation. A thirteenth-century song informs us that 'Now our horse-clawers [grooms], clothed in pride / They busk them with buttons, as it were a bride'.[19] Henry III passed a law forbidding artificers, artisans and tradesmen to wear buttons made of anything but pewter, bone or wood, a law that Henry VIII thought it necessary to revive in 1550.[20] Buttons also seem to have been employed earlier and more often in men's dress than in women's.[21] One of the earliest extant pieces of clothing incorporating buttons is a pourpoint, a waistcoat-like doublet with buttons at the front and on the sleeves, that belonged to Charles du Blois (1319–64). Calvin explicitly condemned men for their wearing of buttons, bellowing in a sermon 'Whereas men doe commonly weare brooches, buttons, & such other thinges, & women weare billiments of gold and other costly attyres vpon their heades: the attire of the faithful must be to haue some remembrance of Gods law'.[22]

Buttons became everyday during the 1600s, and their forms, uses and diameters expanded hugely during the following century. Once again, it was men's costume that led the way, with the rows of buttons that abounded on male waistcoats and breeches.[23] Women continued to rely mostly on hooks and laces for fastenings, but began to mimic men's decorative buttons from the later eighteenth century onwards, when buttons began to be mass produced, principally in Birmingham (button-making remained a craft rather than an industry in France). But during the nineteenth century there was another development which reinforced the association between men and buttons, namely their prominence in the military uniforms that began to be standardised in the early nineteenth century and the many civilian uniforms that imitated them – pages, hotel commissaires, firemen, railway and bank officials, chauffeurs, airline pilots and policemen (known as the 'button-mob' in the US).[24] The figure of 'Buttons' the page in *Cinderella* belongs to this pattern of slightly overreaching male flamboyance. It is for this reason that, odd as it may seem, buttons continue to have male rather than female associations, the button perhaps being to male attire what the pin is to women's. The sign that used to be displayed in male public lavatories in Britain enjoining clients to adjust their dress before leaving is part of the regime of the button rather than the zip fly, aiming as it does to suppress the unsavoury spectacle of men debouching into the street while still fumbling suggestively at their crotches.

If I'm susceptible to buttons, perhaps it's because they were so prominent in the bluecoat uniform worn at my (and Coleridge's) school, Christ's Hospital – seven silver buttons running from neck to waist of the tunic, with the lower coat flaring away to the ankles, along with three buttons worn on the outsides of the knee breeches. These buttons are as symbolically potent as they are conspicuous. The highest rank one can achieve in the school is that of 'Button Grecian', an honour given mostly for academic achievement. A Grecian was a student in the final year, and to become a Button Grecian, or to 'get your buttons', meant that you were permitted to wear a coat adorned with (I am guessing) twice the number of buttons down the front. This expression chimes with one in use in the

Wrens Naval College, where 'getting one's buttons' means being promoted from leading hand to petty officer and thus getting brass uniform buttons in place of black.[25] Though the blue coat has been in use since the foundation of Christ's Hospital in 1553, the first mention of provision for brass buttons is in 1706. The heightened potency of buttons on the coat and breeches contrasts with the complete absence of buttons to secure the shirt and clerical bands still worn by the boys, which are secured now, as they have been for centuries, by pins. It's testimony to the importance of the pin that an unprincipled Matron at Christ's Hospital was accused in 1736 of appropriating for her own profit no fewer than 207,082 of them.[26]

But the button had to wait until the twentieth century for its real transfiguration to take place. For this was the push-button century, in which, steadily taking over from switches, levers and knobs, buttons, which required only to be pressed, became the means of operating hundreds of machines and devices – doorbells, lights, hoovers, telephones, elevators, washing machines, cameras, cars, cisterns, radios, explosives, rockets. The button became the image of the convertibility of scales, the possibility of setting in train or discontinuing a massive, complex and ramifying set of operations by a single elementary motion, one that is almost indistinguishable from pointing. The button was the proof of the new dominion of the miniature, the maximal condensed into the minimal. The button allows the concentration of will and purpose into a single form, a single, simple gesture, and the closing of the gap between intention and action. As the design of buttons developed, there was less and less effort involved in their operation – pressing and pushing buttons gave way to equipment that could be set in motion 'at the touch of a button'. The button was uncoupled from its physical matrix, in order that it could be coupled to a set of powerful, remote and invisible effects. Alarm buttons started to be coloured an inflammatory red, reminding us of their physical origins in the skin, in order to warn of the consequences that could be unleashed by an ill-considered push. During the anxious days of the Cold War, the terrifying ease with which a nuclear war could be begun was focused in the fantasy of a button that somewhere would be pressed to launch the missiles and institute the end of the world. Buttons have migrated to the digital world, where their function is no longer to minimise physical effort but to furnish a compensatory hallucination of it, in the animated images that obediently seem to recess into the screen as you click on them. The unnecessary button proves to be stubbornly irreducible. It continues to require and to conjure a ghostly kind of body, to retain the possibility that we could still bear down on things.

4

Cards

**We are accustomed** to marvelling at miniaturisa-
tion – the ship in a bottle, the bible inscribed on a
crystal, angels dancing on a pinhead. Our aston-
ishment at how small things can now be, and how
laughably lumbering and encumbered the past
was, lugging around its family bibles and brick-
like mobile phones, has become a routine response. What may get
missed in our contemporary, compulsory nano-astonishment is the
more specific kind of magic we work and that works upon us by
thin things. Miniaturisation implies reduction in all dimensions
equally; thinness implies reduction only of one dimension – whether
in the fibre that is spun out, or the substance that is flattened. In
either case, the form or substance in question seems always to have
become charged with potential, which always means that time has
in some way been squashed into space, been put under some kind of
tension. The word 'thin' derives ultimately from an Indo-European

root *tenus*, to stretch, and belongs to a huge family of words signifying various kinds of stretching or straining, including 'tone', 'tune', 'tense', 'tender' and 'attention'. And, within the universe of the thin, there is an even more particular form of magic that is concentrated upon the flat. I am going to try to convince you that the one object that seems to carry all the many powers and associations of the flat is the card, in all its many forms.

Flatness is in fact the strangest and the most exotic of conditions, one that we must have recourse to quite fancy geometry to understand. To be entirely flat, to have only width and breadth but no height at all, is really only accessible to a mathematical comprehension. Edwin A. Abbot's satirical novella *Flatland* offered us the idea of a world restricted to two dimensions as a fable.[1] But this flat world is no mere phantasm. It lives and spreads, more and more emphatically, in our world, with the radical flattening and thinning of computer screens and other devices, which put extravagantly on display the fact that there are no workings going on behind or underneath them. Such flatness has always, so to speak, bulked large in any world that has called itself modern. The flat world is all apparent. It is that world which 'clung together by its edges' of which the philosopher William James speaks.[2] It is the world of the map and the grid and the network; in a network, there is only the lateral slide or knight's move sideways to another site, another page, another screen, which is the same screen. But, above all, flatness inheres in the paper world that has been for so long our own and that we now fear or dream may be passing away.

Flatness is affectless: flatness belongs with depression and the dissociation of autism and schizophrenia. But the flatness of the autistic or schizophrenic world may also be hotly impassioned, however that passion may hide itself, and hide from itself. Flatness is also implicated in certain kinds of representation the purpose of which is to heighten or sustain feeling: the flatness of religious icons, for conspicuous example, helps to give hieroglyphic power; and the flatness of pornographic writing, its obsessiveness and circularity, and especially its transformation of feeling into number, intensity into quantity, seems to account for its simultaneous qualities of pattern and intensity. The *Alice* books and the flat world of cartoons reveal that the flat world is not just associated with stillness and cleanness and delicacy, but also with violence. In cartoons, the flatness of the screen, and the weightlessness of the world it displays, are agitated by an intense violence, a violence that alternates between rupture of bodily forms and flattening of them: Tom the cat is run through a mangle or rolled out like pastry by a road-roller. Though opposites in one sense, the dismemberings and flattenings, the splinterings and spreadings, the contractions and explosions of bodies in the cartoon world are in fact continuous with each other – they are all held together on the taut, unrupturable hypostasis of the cartoon world, the flat laterality against which all is displayed. Ordinary bodies, living vulnerably and decayingly in time, are poised unstably between these two conditions: the atomised and the flattened.

Flatness is the condition of all the ways in which we make sense of the world, taking its voluminous condition and projecting it upon two-dimensional surfaces of different kinds – the page, the canvas, the screen, the chessboard. We say that we 'lay our cards on the table' which is the ideal flat surface in which things may be brought together, for ordering or inspection. This affinity between cards and tables suggests that cards are in fact floating components of some ideal, all-encompassing table of correspondences. The function of the table is to allow the vast, strewn-about jigsaw of the world to be brought together and sorted. To tabulate is to bring the world to the table. The Roman repository of public records was known as a 'tabulary', and the idea lingers in the idea of 'keeping tabs' on something. When the first anatomies began to map out the body, reading it like a book, they anticipated the operating table on which the body would be laid out for observation and repair as a consequence of their knowledge. Even books themselves, which are already a reduction of the world to a flat condition, can be subject to a further round of squashing flat by what became known as a 'table of contents'. The physical table is the scene of, and the approximation to, the schematic arrangement of the world.

A table has two functions. One is that of synthesis or bringing together into one proximate space, of what may be widely separated in the world. A table is the fat world made flat – abstracted, anatomised, amalgamated, anagrammed. But tables are also objects in the world, which means they can themselves be dispersed through it. The Tables of the Law on which Moses inscribed his commandments derive their authority from the fact that they govern everything in the world. But the tables themselves are also worldly and thus subject to the world's accidents and assaults – they can, like the Mosaic tables, be broken, for example.

From early times, a 'tablet' has named a form of mobile table, one that goes out into the world rather than bringing the world to it. A tablet is a small slab on which images or inscriptions could be represented; it has also been used to mean a notebook, and, more recently, a touch-sensitive screen on which one may write. The word 'tablet' has undergone a passage from the world of knowledge to that of the body. Tablets are now more usually not read or written on, but ingested. But, in the swallowing of a tablet, which may often be stamped with some mark, device or information, there may perhaps be some wispy memory of the folkloric idea of literally affixing to or taking into the body some powerfully magic word or written formula; some tablets were in fact designed to be worn around the neck as an amulet. A tablet is the mobile fragment of a table, a table sent out into the world to do its annunciatory or legislating work.

There seem to be certain kinds of objects whose mission is to embody the powers of flatness, which we may identify as the tabulating power of abstracting and reshuffling the world. Such objects are always characterised by the duality of being objects that bring the world together into one place even as they are also objects in the world. They are outside the world which is also outside them. The most powerful, and the most widely disseminated, of the objects which undergo this oscillation is the card. Let us say that cards are the apotheosis of the flat, and the tabulating power that it gives.

The card has been at the centre of the automatic processes that govern the modern world. The first and, before the electronic cards of the present period, the most important and influential form of card was the punched card, which was first used by Jean-Baptiste Falcon in 1726 to automate the process of weaving; the holes punched in wooden cards either allowed or prevented the passage of a thread, thus mechanically determining a design. A hundred years later, Charles Babbage employed cards punched with holes to record information, in his plans for the Analytical Engine, the prototype for the first computer. Punched cards were used in the computations for the US census in 1890, in a system designed by Herman Hollerith. Subsequently, punched cards became ubiquitous during the twentieth century, used in pianolas and other musical automata, by railroads, insurance companies and government agencies of all kinds, and formed the basis for all the most advanced forms of information processing up until the end of the Second World War.[3] Hole punchers were still used to programme computers in living memory (mine), and are still in use in some places to record attendance at work and validate travel tickets. The most important feature of the punched card was that it unified the voluminous chaos of approximate human interactions and the flat world of information. The many forms of the card – on which in the US the warning 'Do not fold, spindle or mutilate', meaning, in essence, 'Keep This Flat', became enigmatically canonical – were the agencies of this communication between the fat and the flat.

This is another way of saying that cards are the visible sign of the communication between an unordered and an ordered world, a world of mingled and overlapping hybrids, and a world sorted into categories. Of course, like other forms of automated inscription and transcription – the groove of the gramophone disc, for example – the punched card was illegible. But the ordering of the world into abstract either/or patterns by means of cards was answered by the passion that grew up during the twentieth century for the collecting of cards of various kinds. The use of trade cards for advertising particular commercial services had grown up during the eighteenth century, though the earliest examples are to be found in the collection made of printed ephemera by Samuel Pepys, now in Magdalene College, Cambridge. There are forty-one of these cards, most of them engravings imitating the shop signs of the businesses in question, including an optician, a milliner, a surgical instrument maker, several tobacconists and, sublime *mis-en-abime*, a card advertising the work of Abraham Faulcon, a playing-card maker.[4] Early trade cards were in fact quite large and likely to be printed on good quality paper; they often served as receipts.[5] It was not until the early nineteenth century that these tradesmen's bills began to be made of stiffened pasteboard, perhaps to survive the rigours of being passed from hand to hand. The explosion of consumer goods and services during the late nineteenth century, and the development of cheap lithographic processes during the 1820s, followed by colour printing, produced a flood of trade cards advertising every conceivable kind of commodity and commercial service – snuff, drugs, dresses, drinks, boot polish, hair dye – but with a particular emphasis on household items – soaps, flat irons and sewing machines.[6] Following the huge expansion of the periodical press from the 1890s onwards, many businesses transferred their advertising from free-standing cards to magazines.[7] From this period on, cards began to be given away as extras with products such as cigarettes and confectionery. During this period, it became apparent that issuing such cards in themed series, either to tell a story (episodic stories like the adventures of Baron Munchhausen were popular), or to gather together representative examples of a particular category of subject – stage beauties, ships, kings and queens, military heroes, aeroplanes, film stars, dogs, cats, flowers – would encourage the desire to collect the set, and thus stimulate more sales. The commodity thus piggybacks on the impulse to bring the world together, to fold successive time back into flat tabulation, which in its turn stimulates serial repetitions in time. The passion for collecting cards – cigarette cards, trade cards, pre-paid telephone cards – is motivated in part by the fact that cards are themselves already collections of data.

There were many different formats, including oval-shaped cards and cards made of materials like silk instead of coloured pasteboard.

There were jigsaw cards, and card games that one could collect. Carter's Little Liver Pills issued a set of dominoes in the 1920s.[8] There was even a series of miniature gramophone records issued as a series of twenty-five 'talkie' cards by the Record Cigarette Company of London. The most highly developed cards in the UK came to be those issued by makers of cigarettes and tobacco products, with a particular emphasis on soccer players. In the early 1900s, there were around 150 different UK tobacco companies issuing cards.[9] During the twentieth century, especially in the US, a new market was found among teenage purchasers of bubblegum and other sweet products, with baseball cards being their staple giveaway. The operation was conducted on a massive scale: Wills's *Railway Engines* series of 1936 had a print run of 600 million.

Merely collecting the set was only the beginning. Collections of cards suggested many different possibilities for secondary applications. One fan of baseball cards evokes some of these:

> The possibilities for variation were practically limitless. You could play games with them on rainy afternoons, using the pictures as surrogate ballplayers. You could arrange and rearrange them in various categories and make lists of all your multiple arrangements. By position, by team, by batting average. By number, by achievement, by personal preference. You could invent various individual rating systems, make trades, construct dream teams, determine strategy.[10]

The most thrilling use of a stiff card was (and, if you ask me, still is) to attach it with a clothes peg to the frame of a bicycle so that the spokes of the rotating wheel flip it as they pass, reproducing perfectly the whirring rattle of a two-stroke engine. The flattened world was not inert, but dizzyingly dynamic. The desire to collect produced a secondary market of exchanges and purchases, so that trade cards (cards issued to help promote trade) became trading cards (cards issued in the hope of stimulating a market in cards themselves). In 1927, the London Cigarette Card Company was founded by Colonel C. L. Bagnall, to put the practice of 'cartophily', the word he coined, on an organised basis. The London Cigarette Company issued catalogues, ran auctions and supplied aids for collectors, such as the magazine *Cigarette Card News* which began publication in 1933. The most valuable trading card in human history so far has been the 'Gretzky T206 Wagner' issued by the American Tobacco Company between 1909 and 1911 and depicting Honus Wagner of the Pittsburg Pirates, which was sold at auction in 2007 for $2.35 million. The pedigree and peregrinations of this aristocratic card have been the subject of much speculation and fabulation and have even prompted a full-blown biography.[11]

The second most important feature of the card, after its thinness, is its stiffness. The stiffness of card is the source of a special kind of ambivalence. Stiffness has many negative associations, for stiffness is the defeat of life by the rigour of death; so a 'stiff' is a corpse, while a 'stiffy' is a name for a stupid person. Stiffness also suggests deceptiveness. To 'stiff' somebody means to con or fool them, perhaps because it reduces them to the condition of a stiff. A 'stiffy' is also a name for a beggar who pretends to be paralysed, for a horse that has no chance of winning, or even of running, and a forged cheque or banknote.

But stiffening also signifies the way in which the living can affirm or augment itself, borrowing the strength of the inanimate world. Thus Henry V exhorts his soldiers at Harfleur to 'stiffen the sinews'.[12] There is a kind of uprightness, a quasi-animate erectness in the card, that, in standing up for itself, seems to disdain and redeem the flimsy ductility of paper. In the card, *rigor mortis* can suddenly spring into *vigor mortis*. Formal invitation cards used to be known to eager English debutantes as 'stiffies'. Where paper merely receives and carries an inscription, a card announces it. The word 'placard' originally referred to a proclamation that had been in some way plated, or stiffened, whether through the application of a seal, or coated with some sticky substance. During the early nineteenth century, placards tended to become less official – advertisements rather than public announcements – and 'placard-men', the forerunners of sandwich-board men, were employed to carry them. When the practice of carrying placards became common in political demonstrations, a custom recalling the heraldic practice of proclaiming one's identity on one's escutcheon, the subordination of the carrier to the message they carried in the form of placard became more emphatic than ever because it was now voluntary.

Perhaps it is because the card seems so charged with this kind of enigmatic second life that cards have become so shuffled in with our identities. A 'charge card' is so-called because one can charge bills to it, but this goes along with the fantasy that attaches to cards, in common with many magical objects, that they themselves carry a store or cargo of power. This power resides not just in 'identity cards', as such; it is also in all the forms of personal validation and accreditation that we now assign to different kinds of card. This began before the age of bureaucracy, in the nineteenth century, in the form of *cartes de visite*, small cards, 3½ × 2 inches (the usual size of cards left when one visited friends, hence the name), on which photographic portraits were printed, and which could be sent to family and friends. The craze for *cartes de visite* swept across Europe from 1854, when they were first patented, to the late 1860s.

But it is with credit cards that we have our most complex and intimate transactions. Edward Bellamy imagined, in his 1888 novel *Looking Backwards 2000–1887*, that in the future every citizen would be issued with a card that was good for a certain proportion of the national product that had been assigned to him. His idea, however, was that such transactions would obviate the complexities of debt and interest payments.[13] The arrival of cards with embedded magnetic strips in 1970 made for the first 'smart cards', cards that encoded information and were capable of forms of interaction. Cards were beginning to come to a sort of magical life.

All of these associations come together in the animated playing cards of *Alice in Wonderland*. Lewis Carroll seems to have had a deep understanding of the dynamics of flatness. The playing-card characters are both less and more alive than Alice. 'Why, you're nothing but a pack of cards!' she snorts, but the very flatness of the characters actually seems to highlight their edgy, abstract savagery.[14] The playing-card characters are more than cards because they are nothing but them. The effect of being ironed flat seems to have made these kings, queens and knaves all sharp knees and elbows. Their flatness also involves the cruelty of the edge – which is to say, the blade of either/or: the Red Queen's axe and her murderous 'Off with their heads!' is her harmlessness ('nothing but a pack of cards') set on edge. The edge is what is unencompassable in the flat card. It is the possibility of turning, the turn of the card on which so much may depend. It is the reversibility, in an utterly flat world, of large and small, of death and inconsequence.

There is danger in the very negligibility of cards; the house of cards became the obvious metaphor for dangerously uncontrolled financial speculation on a global scale. The house of cards is an obvious metaphor for something that can easily come tumbling down. But the impulse to build houses of cards registers the sense that cards, having begun in the reduction of the world from three dimensions to two, always aspire to enter back into the round, substantial world. In this, once again, the most important thing about a playing card is that it has edges. A playing card can be supported by its edges, resting against another card at an angle. The edges of playing cards are what give them their magic possibility of becoming architecture. The world record for card-building is held by the emblematically named Bryan Berg, who built a tower almost 26 feet tall.

I just said that cards aspire to three dimensions, but, given the hold on the future that credit cards give us, and the hold of the future on us, one might say four. The fact that cards seem so charged with life is no doubt bound up with the power which they have seemed to many people to possess, not only to collect together the existing world, but also to hold in store coming events. Cartomancy, or the use of cards for divination, seems to have grown up alongside the use of cards for gaming, with some excitedly insisting that the playing cards in use throughout the world derive from a set of symbols in which ancient Chinese sages preserved their ancient wisdom in secret during times of invasion.[15] Many systems of card magic have been developed, among the more picturesque being the 'Surrealist Racing Forecast Cards' marketed by English artist and minor mystic Austin Spare in 1937.[16] The general magic worked on us by cards is made literal and manifest in the privileged role of card tricks in conjuring.

Playing cards are known as 'flats', a word which has also been applied to the gullible victims of the operations of 'card sharps'. Indeed the musical pun is literalised in the expression 'playing sharps and flats', meaning engaging in the tricking of fools. There is also an interesting commerce between flatness and skin in gaming slang. The victim of a cheating or a fixed game is said to have been 'skinned' in the sense of fleeced. Losing your shirt may be another version of this idea. The term 'skin-faro' refers to a cheating version of the game, in which the dealer takes up two cards rather than one.[17] Eric Partridge gives us a 'skin-house' for a gambling den, and a 'skin-game' for any game that is fixed.[18] Although it is possible to be 'skinned' in any rigged game, whether it be dice or roulette, or any other game involving stakes, the transference of the metaphor from the process to the means of the process is easier when the medium is playing cards. For cards resemble the paper money, the movement of which they bring about, more than any other form of gaming. Indeed, it may be that the suspicion that attached to the introduction of paper money, that conspicuously weightless form of transaction, borrowed its sense of the dangerous impalpability and anonymity of paper from the card table.

So card playing involves a generalised thought of skin, thought thinned to the hectic flatness of skin, and the risk of being reduced by trickery to the condition of the dupe or 'flat'. Gambling and gaming mean tabular life, life rased to an ecstatic plane. Gambling flattens and emaciates its victims, like consumption, as evoked by Callimachus, the opponent of gambling who is given what is meant to be the clinching arguments in Jeremy Collier's *Essay Upon Gaming* of 1713: 'Things lose their Strength and Complexion, and grow lean and languishing … the Hectick comes forward to a galloping Consumption, and the Symptoms appear mortal'.[19] Women were thought during the eighteenth century to be particularly at risk from overindulgence at the table. Gaming is represented often as a sort of anorexia, reducing the body's fullness, and in particular the fullness of the female body, and especially during the great wave of female card playing from the mid-seventeenth century to the end of the eighteenth, to helpless, spectral flatness. As Richard Steele reported:

> [T]here is nothing that wears out a fine Face like the vigils of the Card Table, and those cutting Passions which naturally attend them. Hollow Eyes, haggard Looks, and pale Complexions, are the natural Indicators of the Female Gamester. Her Morning Sleeps are not able to repair her Midnight Watchings. I have known a Woman carried off half dead from Bassette and have, many a time grieved to see a Person of Quality gliding by me, in her Chair, at two a Clock in the Morning, and looking like a Spectre amidst a flare of Flambeaux.[20]

We are often told that the distinguishing feature of the human hand is its opposable thumb, and more specifically the fact that the thumb and index finger can be pressed together, enabling all kinds of actions from turning of screws to the flipping of coins and the stitching of lace. The two dimensions of depth and length of the card both seem to figure this opposable relation. Held between finger and thumb, the thinness of the card is a minimal membrane, an all-but nothing, that seems to be nothing but the difference between front and back, recto and verso. Held by its edges, the card suddenly reveals its spring and resistance, its unsuspected kinetic energy and coiled violence.

Cards also have a mimetic closeness to and intimate involve-ment with the life of the hand which no other form of gambling possesses. The playing card is designed to be held in the hand, and mimes its form. We speak of a hand of cards, and one of the earliest disciplines that must be acquired by every card magician is that of palming, or concealing a card in the palm while the back of the hand is presented to the viewer. The reversing of this process, trans-ferring a card from the front of the hand to the back, is known as 'back-palming'. This suggestion of mirror-imaging on the human hand, as an abstracted redoubling of the body, with its front and its back at once complete opposites of, and yet also in intimate com-munity with, each other, is what gives playing cards their particular kind of strange life. Cards are hand-in-glove with us, they are hand-iwork, they are a kind of image or abstract of the hand itself.

Playing cards are also magical partly because they are meaning-less in themselves; their power only comes from the signs they carry, and the meaning of those signs in relation to other signs. The mean-ing of the playing card is in part its arbitrariness, its flatness, its lack of intrinsic life or meaning, the fact that no card means anything on its own. Its flatness signifies this dry semioticity. Its life comes from contingency and adjacency, from what occurs when it is laid next to another card. In this emptiness of intrinsic form or purpose, the card again resembles the hand itself. But card tricks all depend upon the transfer of the conceptual magic of the card to the physical plane, by making the card or deck seem to come to life as a physical object. The card, or run of cards, which should be empty and flat, deriving their meaning entirely from what is made of them, develop autonomous powers. One of the commonest tricks employed by magicians is the forcing of an apparently free choice. This involves presenting the subject of the trick with a fanned-out pack, face down, with the invitation to pick out any card. Surprisingly, if the magician nudges forward a particular card, seeming to offer it, there is a good chance that it will be accepted. In seeming to be offered, or rather to offer itself, in this way, gesturing or pointing to itself, the card signifies flat paper taking on the life of the hand, palming off on us the prestige of the prestidigitator.

5

Combs

 **I keep my comb** in my back pocket (the right). It is a plain, black, plastic comb, the kind with no handle, but rather a thin ridge in which its springy teeth (exactly ninety, I have just told them off with my thumbnail) are set. It is among the five or six things that I feel I need to have about me at all times. I say 'it', but it has been replaced many times. The fact that I keep it in the same pocket as my wallet means that I have the constant reassurance that it is there. It is a little large for the pocket, so juts out enough to give me a confirming poke when I sit down. Whenever I reach for my wallet, I press against the top edge of the comb with my thumb, sometimes pushing it down just a little if it has ridden up. It becomes a little concave following the curve of my rump, if I have been sitting for a long time, so I periodically pull it out and reinsert it the other way round to bend it back the other way. But its springiness means that it is also easy for it to get hitched

in my wallet when I pull it out to pay for something, and then be catapulted away, or slither across the ground. It is never long, though, before I realise that I am without it. When I do, it is with a little prod of irritable unease followed by a period of mild, wholly tolerable, but still vaguely gnawing bereavement. This never has to last long either, for the reason why my comb is so plain and anonymous is precisely so that it is easily replaced; it seems that any tobacconist or drugstore in almost any city of the world will stock combs of pretty much the same design. I do not insist that it is exactly the same (though now I know that there are ninety teeth in the one I currently have, I suppose I might have to start taking this into account). Nor am I an obsessive comber, for my hair, which is fairly short, rather fine and entirely tractable, does not require a great deal of management. But I feel I want to be equipped to attend to it if the need arises. I comb my hair in the morning, after showering at the gym, before giving lectures and, strangely, on retiring to bed. To be combed and curried is to be prepared, more, to be renewed, to have something in store. It is to have unpicked just a little bit of chaos, inched just a little upstream of time, backed just a little up the slope from entropic tangle and tousle.

To be human is to be combed and combing is perhaps the primary form of adornment or self-fashioning among primates. How old is combing? Combs themselves are at least 12,000 years old, and it seems that every civilisation of which we have records or remains has had them. Sikhs are enjoined to comb their hair twice a day with the khanga (wooden comb), using it to secure their topknot, at the highest point of their heads, as a reminder of the need for discipline and cleanliness, and retying their turban after each ministration. For many human groups, to relinquish the use of the comb is to fall or ritually to step outside the condition of the human. Hindus are enjoined not to brush or comb the hair during periods of mourning. Arawak girls were reported not to be allowed to comb their hair during their first period, until their mother had combed it for them.[1] However, mystics and religions in their early, ecstatic phases often laud the uncombed condition, especially in males. The second-century Clement of Alexandria thought that the male combing of hair was as effeminate as dyeing, and roared that 'their feminine combing of themselves is a thing to be let alone ... for one who is a man to comb himself and shave himself with a razor, for the sake of fine effect, to arrange his hair at the looking-glass, to shave his cheeks, pluck hairs out of them, and smooth them, how womanly!' Clement seems to have seen the difference between men and woman in terms of the difference between the smooth and the crested: while 'God wished women to be smooth', men are like 'cocks, which fight in defence of the hens [which] he has decked with combs, as it were helmets; and so high a value does God set on these locks, that He orders them to make their appearance on men'.[2] So, for Clement, men should not use combs, because in some sense they *are* them.

There are two phases in combing. First one combs out, removing knots and tangles, and making the hair flat, smooth and regular. But then the comb can be used to reintroduce the complexities it has removed, only now in the form of an ordered edifice rather than a random scramble. The comb moves from chaos, through the maximum redundancy of the *tabula rasa*, to ordered complexity. It separates, disarticulates, but then reshapes, introducing designed complication, curling, crimping, bunching, parting, twisting, rebuilding through backcombing. It is as though one took a pack of shuffled cards, sorted them into suits and sequences, then recomplicated them. It is exactly the sequence of operations involved in weaving, which begins with the matted fabric in its natural state, which is then carded or teased (from Latin *carduus* and *teazel*, both meaning a thistle), that is, separated into long and even strands, which are then in turn twisted or woven together, in a kind of higher synthesis. Combing is caught up in the creation, among humans, of the second life, or second body of clothing. Somewhere between a tool and a garment, a comb is the most intimate form of body furniture.

However, though one might associate combing with the human arts of weaving, combing and grooming behaviour is extremely widespread among furred, feathered and bristled creatures, the instrument of grooming nearly always being some other part of the body, the paw, the claw, the bill or the tongue (cats have a thistle-like tongue that ideally combines the functions of comb and scratcher). Human beings continue to see the world in terms of fur and fabric, with our hair the bearer of the awareness we can never quite relinquish of our vanished pelts. We are ruffled, rubbed up the wrong way, have our teeth set on edge; we run into snags and hitches, sometimes end up looking as if we have been dragged through a hedge backwards.

Animals do not only comb themselves. Spiders comb out the silk with which they spin the webs that themselves comb the air for their prey, and are then imitated by humans with nets and snares. Worms endlessly plough the earth, and whales sieve the sea for plankton. Trees in certain tropical regions gather water from low-lying fog and cloud in a process known as 'cloud-combing'.[3] Nasal hairs clean and filter the inbreathed air for impurities. The millions of alveoli in the lungs comb the air for oxygen; the intestines extract nutrients from food. The air, so systematically swept by swifts and other aerial predators, can also comb on its own account, as one can see in the sculpting of cliffs and the shaping of dunes. 'Winnowing' originally meant exposing grain to the wind so that the lighter chaff will be blown away, which explains why the word appears in the form 'windowing' until the eighteenth century. Perhaps an individual organism is no more than a particular kind of screen – both a filter and a foregrounding – of its environment. Perhaps what we think of as our conscious self is just a selective intensifier of all the millions of energies and impulses that are traversing us.

The fact that we are primates, creatures in which grooming behaviour is a crucial part of social organisation, means that we constantly comb each other, in the ways in which we filter and feed back to each other. For, if there is something narcissistically fascinating about combing or brushing the hair, all the more since both comb and brush are so often deployed with mirrors, then there is also an embodied limit to this self-palpation. Though we can all comb the backs of our own heads, we cannot see the results of our operations, except in glimpses. It is for this reason that we depend on others for much of our grooming. This gives a new, more sociable sense to the expression 'watch your back', for, seen from this point of view, your back is the dimension of your social existence. Indeed, it has recently been suggested that, far from social grooming being necessary to help keep our hair clean, the fact that, unlike almost all other animals, our hair does not grow to a certain length and then stop, but just keeps on growing indefinitely, suggests that our hair exists in order to provide opportunities for styling and display.[4] Alison Jolly suggests the importance of cooperation in this process:

'Truly untended hair implies that the wearer is desperate or insane and, furthermore, has no friends ... To convey social status or sexual attractiveness it doesn't matter whether you curl, uncurl, braid, blow-dry, or use powder or mud: The signal is that somebody has clearly done something to the bits round the back'.[5]

The comb's primary function is to group and sort. It creates what is known as a laminar flow, in which layers in a stream flow in absolutely parallel lines, without bending or crossing over. Laminar flows can exert enormous force – laminar flow over the curved top surface of an aeroplane wing, for example, is what creates the pressure differential that lifts the plane into the air. Turbulence, which occurs when the lines of the flow start to get tangled up, reduces the efficiency of the aeroplane dramatically. Laminar flow is stable and calculable; it represents nature combed and filtered into orderly correspondence; turbulence is unkempt (literally 'uncombed') and unpredictable. J. G. Frazer recorded a number of superstitious beliefs about combing the hair being the cause of torrential downpours; one might have expected the knot or tangle to be more suggestive of storm, but the emphasis here seems to be on the magical power of unloosing involved in combing.[6] (Surprisingly, though, 'filter' comes from the word 'felt', which signifies a packed and matted material; the best filter is often itself a densely reticulated tangle.) Turbulence is in fact nearly everywhere, and still represents one of the greatest challenges to physics. Horace Lamb, one of the founders of the science of fluid dynamics, is said to have remarked to a meeting of the British Association in London in 1932 'I am an old man now, and when I die and go to Heaven there are two matters on which I hope for enlightenment. One is quantum electrodynamics and the other is the turbulent motion of fluids. And about the former I am really rather optimistic'.[7] By contrast, laminar, or combed, flow, so compliant with our calculations, is in fact very rare indeed in nature. Parallel lines, that, as Euclid tells us, meet only at infinity, seem to offer the intersection of this infuriatingly approximate, not-quite world with the absolute. Is it perhaps the other-worldliness of the laminar that makes the human (and animal) desire to comb things out so intense and unresting, sublimely restful though the process of combing is in itself?

Combing certainly has strong associations with magic and the supernatural. Many Irish legends of the Banshee, the wailing or singing messenger of death, show her combing her hair as she sings: stealing her comb brings dire consequences.[8] Hairs harvested from combs, like nail clippings, can place you in the power of the sorceror. Snow White is put into her deathly coma by a poisoned comb. Combs can also harbour more benign powers. There is a story that, following the death of Alcuin of York, the eight-century scholar, one of his followers found that a touch of his master's comb miraculously cured his migraine. Another disciple found that touching the teeth with the comb provided similar relief from toothache.[9]

The filtering that combing involves is at work in a huge number of human operations and techniques. Early-morning visitors to Continental beaches will be in time to see the tractors which rake the sand into immaculate condition for the new day, beachcombing in the most literal sense. The obsessive cult of the lawn among Anglo-Saxon peoples requires endless raking and the combing effect of the mower, leaving its visible stripes like the tracks of an enormous comb. During the Second World War, the tactic of turning a ship or submarine parallel with the approaching tracks of torpedoes to reduce the likelihood of being hit became known as

'combing the tracks'. Ever since I saw the bones in the Paris cata-
combs neatly sorted and stacked into shins, femurs and clavicles, I
have always, though with no etymological warrant, thought of the
word 'catacomb' as embodying a sort of charnel-house combing.

Filtering is a crucial component, not only of human techniques,
but also of the forms of human understanding. In common with
many other creation myths, the biblical story of Genesis begins, not
with creation *ex nihilo*, but with acts of divine sorting and separation, first of all dividing the light from the darkness, then the heaven
from the earth, and then the earth from the sea (Genesis 1:4–10).
Evolutionary theory suggests a different explanation for the emergence of life, though one that still involves the work of filtering, in
which environmental conditions comb the random mutations
thrown up by errors in the transmission of the DNA code in order
to select natural forms that fit or line up with those conditions.
Cosmology repeats cosmogony: in April 2008, Chih-Hao Li of the
Harvard-Smithsonian Center for Astrophysics announced a technique he had developed known as astro-combing, which uses ultra-
short laser pulses as a filter to show up the tiny variations in starlight
spectra that signal the gravitational tugs imparted to stars by planets.[10] And as above, so below: MRI, magnetic resonance imaging,
works by magnetically combing the hydrogen protons in the subject's body, or aligning them all in the same direction; variations in
the rate at which protons resume their polarities after the magnetic
field is turned off indicate variations in the tissue, such as tumours.
In mathematics, a 'sieve' is the name for an algorithmic procedure
that obtains a particular sequence of numbers by systematically
eliminating or sieving out unwanted numbers. The most famous of
these is the sieve of Eratosthenes, which is a procedure for

determining all prime numbers, by removing, from the number sequence 1, 2, 3, etc, first all multiples of 2 (the first prime number), then all multiples of 3 (the next prime), then of 5 (the next), then of 7, and so on. The numbers that are left will all be primes.

Filtering is also involved in the making out of other forms, especially in sound. When we listen to language, we filter out all the meaningless noise from what our language picks out as the phonetically meaningful units of sound. Filtering is also involved in the production and perceptual distinguishing of music; Emily Dickinson evokes 'that old measure in the Boughs – / That phrase-less Melody – / The Wind does – working like a Hand, / Whose fingers Comb the sky'.[11] The lines produced by the comb have a suggestion of the parallel lines of the musical score, and, of course, the comb is also capable of producing its own music, in the peculiar allotrope of the human voice it offers in the kazoo or comb and paper. The Rhine maidens sat upon the Lorelei rock and lured mariners to death by singing as they combed their foam-like locks with golden combs. Mermaids endlessly comb their hair, perhaps, because they are themselves the emanation of the sea surf, which poetic tradition often represents as combing itself: the mermaid is the sea spontaneously combed into semi-human form.

Listening closely to a polyphonic piece of music may involve a kind of parallel processing, as one teases out the different harmonic lines, to enable them to be heard horizontally in their semi-auton-omous simultaneity, rather than in the stacked, vertical condition of their interferences with each other. I wonder whether this mode of parallel thinking could be a model for analogical and metaphorical thinking in general. In the complex forms of such thinking what matters are not relations between objects, but relations between relations. In the form of what is known as a homology, the elementary structure of equivalence is often 'a:b as c:d'; sunset is to sunrise as death is to birth. Nobody could ever read a map or a wiring diagram or a piece of sheet music without this cognitive grammar of extended correspondence. Thinking in parallel lies at the heart of much discovery, argument and invention, not least in the opportunities it offers thought, for example in jokes and laughter, to jump the tracks and pleasingly snarl up the parallel lines.

If one could hear all frequencies, hearing would be simply overwhelmed in white noise. Without some kind of filter, nothing can be seen or known. But a filter necessarily discards or ignores much of what it processes. The vast explosion of information in the modern world makes combs and filters more necessary than ever. A Google search operates under precisely these conditions, in which the very shape of the filter will always conceal as much as it discloses. David William Cohen has pointed to the way in which historical narratives are brought about by this kind of filtering, in which it is possible to remember or recall only at the cost of forgetting. What he calls 'the combing of history' is this necessary "'forgetting" in the "remembering"'.[12]

There are comb-like alignments and spannings everywhere in our world and the worlds we have made. The plough leaves laminar striations as though it were combing the earth, and the written or printed page ('page' coming from *pagus*, a field) follows in the same tracks. The schoolboy who tapes six pens together to expedite the writing of his hundred lines (why is my head still so full of antique wheezes like this?) is employing parallel processing. There are also circular versions of laminar flow, as instanced in the grooves of gramophone records, and the helicoidal packings of the scroll and the reel of tape. Contour lines, the lines of force in magnetic fields, the swirls of isobars in weather systems, the rippling shock waves from an earthquake, the alignments of planets in astrology, and the encapsulated, humming spheres of the Ptolemaic universe, all display this concentricity.

Of course, the impulse to fillet out every irregularity and purify every mixture can take cruel and pathological forms. The sociable grooming instinct can become a blindly autistic compulsion, as for example in obsessive picking and scratching behaviours, and forms of personal and ethnic cleansing can be driven by the impossible and deathly desire to undo or deter any kind of admixture.

Combing is full of odd duplicities and complicities. The first comb was perhaps the hand (and, because the Germans were said to be the last people in eighteenth-century Europe to take to periwigs, the hand was sometimes referred to as 'a German comb') or its fingers (the metacarpus, the fan of bones between the wrist and fingers, used to be known as the 'comb'), so that the comb therefore doubles the hand that deploys it. The comb and the hair then act out a game of reciprocal alignment; the comb follows the lines of the hair, which start to resemble its form, the comb becoming a kind of mirror of the hair it shapes. On the one hand, the comb straightens out and filters, and therefore tends to flatten the hair. On the other hand, the hair that stands up in a crest is itself ridged or toothed like a comb. The erectile relation between the human hair and the cock's comb is a close one. A man or a woman used to be said to be getting 'red in the comb' if they were becoming interested in sex.[13] Fruit flies have bristles that are known as 'sex-combs' on their legs. This alternation between the comb's flattening and tempering effect and the phallic asperity of its form is to be found in the beautiful word 'pexity', which has not been in use since the seventeenth century, from *pexus*, combed, past participle of *pectere*, to comb, which signifies, not so much a combed condition, as the nap, or raised roughness of a fabric.

There are similarly close and reversible relations between teeth and combs. The word *comb* derives from a pre-Teutonic root *gomb-hos*, cognate with Sanskrit *gambhas*, both meaning a tooth. Human teeth themselves can of course act as a comb, an idea that seems to motivate references to the mythical 'tooth-comb', an effect of the mistaken transposition of the hyphen from fine-tooth. Actually, though, the toothbrush performs exactly the function of a tooth comb – a set of teeth that combs another set of teeth. Combing often seems to raise the zebra-stripe conundrum – white stripes on black, or black on white? Does the wind comb the grass, or the grass comb the wind?

Filtering itself is reversible. I can comb dye or conditioner into my hair, just as I can flush nits and lice out by combing. What you rake or sieve out can sometimes be gold and sometimes dross. A rake, in the sense of a reprobate, is short for a 'rakehell', in reference to phrases such as 'if you had raked hell with a fine-toothed comb you would not find such a villain'. This is an odd inversion of the troublesome Christian doctrine of the Harrowing of Hell, which holds that, during the intermission between crucifixion and resurrection, Christ descended into Hell, or the realm of the dead, to redeem Adam and Eve and the prophets. In this case, the selective filter is designed to pluck out saints rather than scoundrels.

Combing or brushing the hair may both soothe and stimulate; when I brush my cat Leila, she cannot help extending her claws and raking the cushion or carpet she is lying on in mimetic redoubling of the action. Combs and brushes are surprisingly lively objects. Combing or brushing your hair in the dark can produce visible sparks; the electrostatic charge in a comb that you have just used is strong enough to deflect a stream of water from a bathroom tap.

Combing is part of a complex spectrum of effects: too light a touch and the comb will make no impression, just as too light a scratch will intensify rather than tackle an itch. A kind of violence always lies implicit within the action of combing: a heckle is an instrument for combing flax; the practice of political heckling comes from a transferred sense of the word, meaning to subject to a searching investigation. The Greeks saw cleaning as inseparable from the abrasive combing of the skin effected by the instrument known as the strigil, a practice remembered in the term 'striges' for the channels or flutings in architectural columns. Too much stimulation eventually becomes painful, leading ultimately to the appalling torture of the judicial machinery known as the Harrow in Franz Kafka's story 'In the Penal Settlement'.[14]

Combing can be delicious, but is often also, as we say, harrowing. A 'crabtree comb' is a cudgel that may be violently applied to the head. In one version of the song of *John Barleycorn*, a story of death and rebirth, combing is part of the torture inflicted on the crop:

> With harrowes strong they combed him
> and burst clods on his head:
> A ioyfull banquet then was made,
> when Barly-corne was dead.[15]

In the late nineteenth century, combs began to be made of synthetic materials, like the celluloid developed by Isaiah and John Hyatt in 1869, which was a mixture of nitro-cellulose and camphor.

These proved occasionally to be as dangerous as the celluloid film for which it was also used, as the material from which they were made, which is chemically very similar to the explosive known as gun-cotton, was highly combustible. The *British Medical Journal* reported in 1897 on a case of a woman badly burned when she bent too close to a candle with a celluloid comb in her hair, and speculated that 'it would seem to be possible for a comb closely confined as it is in the hair to explode without any apparent cause'.[16]

This is perhaps a long way to have travelled from the black plastic comb holstered in my back pocket. I have felt at times, as I have plucked and pinged at its palissade of prongs, like Ingrid Bergman puzzling over the fork lines in a white tablecloth that so distress the amnesiac Gregory Peck in Hitchcock's *Spellbound* (1945). Combs do indeed seem to be things to be sieved and sifted, to be full of rhymes and reasons. Combing through the implications of the comb in this way resembles, in the way in which it interlocks with itself, the evocation of combing at the end of Wallace Stevens's poem 'Of Modern Poetry', which concludes that a poem : 'must / Be the finding of a satisfaction, and may / Be of a man skating, a woman dancing, a woman / Combing. / The poem of the act of the mind'.[17] The poetry of this object is the action it gives to the mind in drawing it into its shape.

It is like one of those nameless objects that cryptically address us in Anglo-Saxon riddles, teasing us with the question 'What am I?' Indeed, Alcuin of York, whom we have met already, is the author of one such riddle. It was written in Latin in thanks for a gift made of ivory sent to him by his friend Archbishop Riculf of Mainz in 794.[18]

Bestia nam subito nostras subrepserat aedes,

At a stroke, a creature crept into our place.
In qua imago fuit capitum miranda duorum;
An amazing sight it was, with its two heads
Quae maxilla tamen pariter coniunxerat una.
joined with just the one jawbone,
Bis ternis decies sed dentibus horruit illa.
though that teemed thick with sixty teeth.

Esca fuit crescens illis de corpore vivo,
Meals from a mortal body (but neither meat nor veg)
Nec caro, nec fruges. Fructus nec vina bibentum
were growing in them. No grog, no grub, got past its
   grinders
Dentibus edebat; patulo non tabuit ore.
yet still, with mouth wide open, it didn't waste away.
Scis, Damoeta meus, quae sit haec bestia talis?
Any clue, Damoeta mate, what kind of creature it could
   be?[19]

The answer is surely not too hard to puzzle out. It is of course a comb, perhaps the very comb that exhibited such curative efficacy after Alcuin's death. Which is to say, the answer to the riddle is in effect – a riddle.

6

Glasses

 **I have worn glasses** for as long as I can remember, indeed, now I come to think of it, for longer even than that. My first pair of glasses, I am informed, was held in place around my infant head with elastic, since my budding nose and ears were insufficiently prominent to support them. My world has, as a consequence, always been a refracted, relayed, conditional thing. There has always been an intermediary in my visual transactions with the world, inciting in me, perhaps, a strongly developed feeling for intercessions of all kinds. For some twenty years I was able to dispense with glasses, with contact lenses doing the job instead. But, with the waning of my reading powers in what may yet turn out to have been my middle age, I have renewed my acquaintance with glasses.

In the intervening time, something has changed. When I was a child, my glasses defined me. I lived through them, I lived in them.

There was little I could do without them; they not only brought the world into focus, they also gave me resolution. They were a kind of emblem or vocation of the kind of child I was – studious, wary, watchful, not very strong or brave. But now, glasses have become a kind of prop, they are optional, stagey, even operatic, dandyish, twinklingly ironic. I feel sure that, like an antique aunt in bombazine, I should know instinctively what to do with a lorgnette (known in Edwardian times as 'starers'). As a child, seeing and looking for me were not actions, they were defining conditions; they were what I needed to do to get around the world. Nowadays, I watch myself putting on shows of looking, exhibitions of attention and inspection; I display myself to myself, and others. Perspicuity has given way to conspicuousness. Like St Lucy, whose martyrdom involved the gouging out of her eyes, and who is therefore often shown in paintings displaying them like scallops on a golden plate, I have my eyes always ready to hand. As a child, I had one pair of glasses, that I clamped over my ears in the morning and only took off to swim or sleep. Having only one pair of glasses meant that I could never see them properly. Without my glasses, I stood no chance of finding them. This meant careful routines of disposition and insurance – the glasses needed always to be in the same place, on the same side of the bed. But now that I have more pairs of glasses than my grandfather had pipes, I can abandon them anywhere. My glasses have entered my field of vision, rather than being it. It is not the eyes that are the windows of the soul, it is glasses and, as in Henry James's house of fiction, the soul, or this one, now has many windows to look out of.[1]

As a teacher, I spend a lot of time listening to people – to students, applicants, suppliants, complainants, administrators, vendors, mentors, mentees. A pair of glasses is an indispensable adjunct to the display of auditory engagement. Deaf old Edwardian ladies used sometimes to indicate their lack of interest in a particularly tedious speaker by conspicuously lowering the mouths of their hearing trumpets downwards to the tabletop. By contrast, I grant people entry to the space of my attention by taking my glasses off. Deployed in this way, spectacles are an absolute necessity for the spectacle of alertness I supply, for myself as well as those about me. Glasses used to be necessary to correct my vision, to bring things to a focus, to let me look, to lock me into the world. Though more than ever optically necessary, glasses are now a means of diversion, play, and display.

My glasses were carefully prescribed for me as a child, and I remember being amused by my father's stories of people in 1920s Merseyside where he grew up rummaging through trays of assorted second-hand spectacles in Woolworths, looking for a pair that wouldn't do too badly for them. But now, when reading glasses are available in various strengths in pharmacists and general stores, one can rely on finding pairs of glasses anywhere, or at least wherever one can find combs. Glasses have become a currency, not least wherewith to perform actions and transactions with ourselves. For glasses concern very much more than our vision; they are closely and expressly involved with many aspects of our bodily life. A pair of glasses is an animator, an intensifier, a magnifier, a focaliser, a distributor and a transformer of the body. It is not just an accessory pair of eyes, but a whole little optical homunculus. When you are as dependent upon glasses as I, they come to seem like your double. When I look at my glasses on the desk, with its, or their, arms, or legs (or ribs?) opened out, they seem to have an elementary phantom of me still lingering inside them, eyes behind the windows, ears pricked. Whether one calls the side pieces of glasses by their technical name of 'temple arms', or, as in Scotland, 'legs', seems to me to change everything about them, somehow. A pair of glasses with arms seems docile and reliable, for it does what arms do, namely holds to me and offers me assistance. A pair of glasses with legs seems much more apt or able to stand on its own two feet, and even walk away.

Like all magical objects, glasses provide an object and occasion for fidgeting. Fidgety behaviour suggests worry and uneasiness, but it is really a way of easing these conditions. The enormous class of things with which we fidget are ways of playing with ourselves at a distance, putting ourselves into serious play. With a pair of glasses, the play may be rather risky – testing the strength or bendiness of the joints, holding them by one arm, or leg – which is part of its point. Play is meant to protect us against the jeopardy which it encounters and enacts. Dangling diagonally from one arm, or leg, gripped in my front teeth, or whirlybirded around with one arm, or leg, they seem helpless and vulnerable, while I feel suavely, sadistically insouciant. Folded, like a crab's claws shutting above its head (and how delicious is the dull clack they make when they do that) they seem firmly, even sulkily, withdrawn.

I like to draw the ear-pieces together and then pinch them, half-open and half-closed, with a thumb and forefinger, making a slightly unstable but agreeable isosceles which I can meditatively heft or waggishly waft about. Sometimes, the joined ear-pieces can be cinched by the top joints of the first and second fingers, curled to form a claw like that of a claw hammer, in a grip not dissimilar to that employed in playing the spoons. The glasses can then be flicked up and down, as though I were a fifties beatnik clicking his fingers to some hot jazz, to mark my oratorical periods, or my mild exasperation at what I may be hearing. The hand-eye-glasses assemblage becomes a sort of manopticon, or seeing hand, which can provide a commentary, docile or sceptical, on whatever is going on around it.

Taking glasses off is altogether easier, and productive of much more powerful theatrical effects, than putting them back on. It is like the problem the stripper faces in the pub with no changing room, when she has to find an elegant way to pick up her strewn togs after the performance is complete. It seems to me that there are essentially two ways of putting glasses back on. The issue is, that if you thrust them straight on to your face, you are liable to prod yourself in the eye with one of the ear-pieces. I am quite accomplished at the rather dashing movement that involves rotating my head slightly to the right, anchoring the left arm, or foot, of the glasses in the little dint in my left temple, then turning my head back to the left so that I am facing the front again, this process serving to stretch the arms apart, like a wishbone, sufficiently to be able to slide the glasses safely back in their channels over the ears. But on the whole I prefer the dignified pathos of the movement that involves holding the glasses apart with two hands in front of and slightly below the level of my face, and then gravely dipping my head towards them, as though I were donning a balaclava, or bowing to be invested with a chivalric order, a movement that feels more like inserting myself inside my glasses than putting them on me. Oh yes: into, out, on, through, from, behind, beside, towards, glasses offer a positive gymnastics of prepositions.

It is not clear where or by whom spectacles were invented,

though we can pin down their appearance fairly precisely to the last two decades of the thirteenth century, probably somewhere in northern Italy. Some attribute their invention to Salvino d'Armati, a Florentine who died in 1317, and whose grave in the Church of Santa Maggiore describes him as 'inventore degli occhiale'. Others have credited Alessandro Spina of Pisa, or Roger Bacon in England.[2] But the principle that one could use convex lenses to correct sight had been understood for centuries before this; Seneca, for instance, explained in around AD 65 that '[l]etters, however tiny and obscure, are seen larger and clearer through a glass ball filled with water'.[3]

The first eyeglasses, using convex lenses, were developed to correct hyperopia, or long-sightedness. Oddly, it took another 150 years for the first glasses to correct myopia, using concave lenses, to be developed (in around 1450). Why might this have been? One plausible suggestion is that the invention of eyeglasses was driven, during the huge expansion of trade and banking in northern Italy in the early Renaissance, by the need to concentrate the workforce in occupations that required close-up work – the crafts of weaving, sewing, carpentry, shoemaking and, most importantly in the late thirteenth century, clerical and accounting functions.[4]

Eyeglasses are associated with feebleness and timidity, but they have also from the earliest times been apt to focus fantasies of secret power. This may be in part because glasses always to some degree mask the eyes they assist. One of the reasons that Roger Bacon is sometimes credited with their invention is because of the references in his work to the powers of magnifying lenses: 'if the following designe be conjoyned to the former (viz.) Glasses so cast, that things at hand may appear at distance, and things at distance, as hard at hand: yea so farre may the designe be driven, as the least letters may be read, and things reckoned at an incredible distance'. Bacon goes on to evoke the marvels of telescopic vision, claiming that Julius Caesar used 'great Glasses from the Coasts of *France*, to view the site and disposition of both the Castles and Sea-Towns in great *Britain*' and that, using lenses, Socrates 'did discover a Dragon, whose pestiferous breathings and influences corrupted both City and Countrey thereabouts, to have his residence in the Caverns of the Mountains'. Even more pleasing, if even less probable, is the suggestion that 'Glasses may be framed to send forth *Species*, and poisonous infectious influences, whither a man pleaseth. And this invention *Aristotle* shewed *Alexander*, by which he erecting the poison of a Basilisk upon the Wall of a City, which held out against his Army, conveyed the very poison into the City it self'.[5]

Some of the earliest reading aids may in fact not have been worn, but laid over books. The earliest 'reading stones', as they were called, date from around AD 1000. This links the optical properties of glass to the magical powers often invested in gems and jewels. Pliny hints at the use of emeralds (or what he calls 'smaragdi') for optical effects, suggesting that the Emperor Nero used them to view gladiators. This may be because they are 'generally concave in shape, so that they concentrate the vision [*concavi ut visum conligant*]'. In fact, Pliny gives these stones a restorative power for the eye, since, uniquely, they feed the eyes without satiating them [*inplent oculos nec satiant*]. What is more, they are self-magnifying, since, says Pliny, they 'appear larger when they are viewed at a distance because they reflect their colour upon the air around them' [*longinquo amplificantur visu inficientes circa se repercussum aëra*].[6]

The belief in the magical powers of spectacles seems to linger. When I was a child, I longed to believe in the small ads in Marvel comics for X-ray spectacles that would allow me to see through walls and ladies' clothing. Since vision is the most active and inter-rogative of the senses, it is hard for humans to believe that its pow-ers cannot be enhanced by sheer willpower, and fantasies of X-ray vision and other modes of clairvoyance abounded long before the discovery of X-rays in 1895.[7] I discovered the physical power of my glasses as a child, for, on a sunny day, I could set carbon paper and pigtails smouldering in a matter of seconds. Piggy, the bespectacled fat boy in William Golding's *Lord of the Flies*, is given the same power over fire (much of the authority of the word 'spectacles', as opposed to the vernacular 'glasses', is surely the way it clicks together with the word 'intellectual'); and the smashing of his glasses later in the novel is the definitive sign of the boys' abandonment of civilised reason for bestial passion. Although it feels right for the studious, asthmatic Piggy to have this Promethean accomplishment, his glasses would not actually have served to concentrate the rays of the sun as mine did, for, as a myope, his lenses would have been concave rather than convex.

Glasses are an indispensable supplement to the work of persua-sion or browbeating. As a leader in *The Times* observed in 1948, prompted by the rush of people to acquire free glasses under the newly instituted National Health Service:

> To the orator, the divine, the advocate, they can add a whole vocabulary, not indeed of words, but of gestures. Many a wit-ness, deeming himself as bold as brass, has been reduced to an abject condition by a pair of pince-nez skilfully

manipulated. They can be waved as a devastating prelude to attack and resumed with a crushing finality. They can be taken off and carefully wiped with an air portending terrible things.[8]

Perhaps the associations of glasses with the desire for power accounts for the fact that, for centuries after they became common, the wearing of spectacles attracted ridicule and suspicion. Fools were frequently shown adorned with or clutching spectacles.[9] The German humanist Sebastian Brant included in his satirical poem *The Ship of Fools* a woodcut showing a bibliomaniac, completely surrounded by his books, clutching a fool's cap and brush and wearing an enormous pair of insect-like goggles.[10] Even today, the simplest and most effective way to disfigure a portrait is to inscribe over it a big, round pair of glasses. To be given spectacles is to be made a spectacle. The suspicions about glasses constitute a hidden counter-tradition to the prevailingly benign view of their effect; in this tradition, glasses are associated with jealousy, craftiness, voyeurism, hubristic desire, blindness, even madness. In what may very well be the first mention of eyeglasses in poetry, in 'Sopra la nuove disposizione del mundo mutate al male' ('On the New Order of the World Turned Bad'), the Florentine poet Franco Sacchetti seems to associate their wearing with financial double-dealing, usury being forbidden at this time (and glasses might be thought to be inherently duplicitous, since they double our eyes – hence 'four-eyes'): 'Artisans, it seems to me, have become as knowledgeable and astute as brokers; they examine the books with spectacles to settle accounts, and with pens on their ears and with disguised interest-bearing loans'.[11] In a satire written against the Jesuits, John Donne elaborately mocked the magic spectacles that apparently make it possible for Ignatian divines to furnish detailed descriptions of the fixtures and fittings of Hell:

> In the twinckling of an eye, I saw all the roomes in Hell open to my sight. And by the benefit of certaine spectacles, I know not of what making, but, I thinke, of the same, by which *Gregory* the great, and *Beda* did discerne so distinctly the soules of their friends, when they were discharged from their bodies, and sometimes the soules of such men as they knew not by sight, and of some that were never in the world, and yet they could distinguish them flying into Heaven, or conversing with living men, I saw all the channels in the bowels of the Earth; and all the inhabitants of all nations, and of all ages were suddenly made familiar to me.[12]

The idea that eyeglasses impose a kind of filter or limit on vision, rather than augmenting it – the idea of seeing the world 'through rose-tinted spectacles' – occurs early, too. A 1496 sermon by the famous Dominican preacher Girolamo Savanarola evokes the distorting effect of different kinds of glasses: 'So if you have good spectacles, you will always see good things, and if they are not good, you will see wicked things … Yellow glasses raise phantoms of envy or of avarice … Red glasses signify rage and vengefulness …You should submit to the rule of the spectacles of death'.[13] In Edgar Allan Poe's story 'The Spectacles', a young man unwittingly marries his great-great-grandmother, and is able to see her horrifyingly aged features only when he puts on a pair of spectacles she gives him.[14] Glasses are even more sinister in E. T. A. Hoffmann's 'The Sandman', in which Dr Coppelius, a maker of automata, is associated both with the stealing of eyes and with the making of spectacles. He comes into the narrator's room and offers him 'beautiful eyes', as he spills out on to the table a pile of sinisterly glinting lorgnettes and glasses:

> 'Now, now, glass-a, glass-a to wear on your nose-a, dese are my eyes-a, beautiful eyes-a!' And with these words he pulled out more and more spectacles, so that the whole table began strangely gleaming and shining. Innumerable eyes flickered and winked and goggled at Nathanael; but he could not look away from the table, and Coppola put more and more spectacles on it, and their flaming eyes sprang to and fro ever more wildly.[15]

There is something potentially cracked or crazy about glasses, never more so than in the Groucho Marx nose, moustache and glasses combo. As Arnauld Maillet has put it, in a play on words that has defeated my efforts to translate it, 'les lunettes peuvent devenir elles-mêmes lunatiques'.[16]

Lifelong wearers of eyeglasses have to get used to a thousand little tricks and freaks that come from the properties of optical glass and plastic. I used to be able to focus on the outside corner of my lens and catch an exquisitely magnified reflection of my own eyelid and eyelashes. For the most part, you see *with* contact lenses; but, with eyeglasses, you see *through* a medium that is always itself noisily visible. Lenses scratch and fog and smear. Wearers of glasses can sometimes be observed walking backwards into pubs, a ritual that is believed to prevent them steaming up. After a warm day I would find a greasy half-moon imprint of my eyebrow on the top edge of each lens. One of the many forms of bodily intuition that glasses have given me is an awareness of the grease transfer index of any item. Because I have a horror of the refractive stripes and bar sinisters that streaks of grease impart to the vision, I have an instinctive understanding of what may be pressed into service as cleaning materials. Freshly laundered handkerchiefs are the best. I am astonished when I see people cleaning their glasses on their ties, or shirttails, or even, my God, between finger and thumb. I imagine them cheerfully swigging from half-empty beer bottles on the street, or offering used tissues around.

Glasses are never simply used or worn; they are, to use Jean-Paul Sartre's expression, *existed* – both lived out and brought into active and magical existence.[17] They are one of the richest and most versatile forms of my self-invention and self-securing. They are an abstract, an anatomy, and an anagram of my being. I live myself out in them, and I can see them seeing me out.

7

Handkerchiefs

 **When the runaway wraps up** his worldly goods prior to taking to the road, it is, of course, invariably in a big spotted handkerchief, which is then hung like a big plum pudding from the end of a stick. What would you possibly put in such a parcel? A hunk of bread and cheese? A pair of boots? Perhaps a spare handkerchief?

The pressed, folded handkerchief has all the glamour of the immaculate (the field of virgin snow, the empty swimming pool, the waiting page). The touch and smell of a cool, freshly opened handkerchief, as it turns from a *tabula rasa* to a billowing tent, in which one might be lapped and lost, is among the most comfortingly voluptuous sensations that this world can afford. The handkerchief is startlingly various in size, and seems to convert and commute between different scales. Handkerchiefs morph into sails and parachutes. The stork brings babies knotted in handkerchiefs. It is not for nothing that large handkerchiefs are called 'man-sized', since the ideal handkerchief would in fact unfold to encompass the whole of a person. The handkerchief or *sudarium* (the sweat cloth) with which Christ's face was wiped becomes the winding-sheet which, like the handkerchief, is miraculously printed with his image. But, when knotted at four corners and worn on the head, when sodden with tears, when balled by anxiety or grief, a handkerchief shrinks to a 'hanky'.

I began by evoking the association of the handkerchief with departure and flight, and this is fitting, for the handkerchief itself seems often to be in transit, from person to person, from place to place and from application to application. 'Drop the Handkerchief' is a chasing game, in which players stand in a ring. The player designated as 'it' walks round the outside of the ring, and drops a handkerchief behind one of the other players, who must then try to chase and catch him or her before thay can complete a circuit and take the chaser's place in the circle. As in the game of 'Buttony' I described earlier, the point of the handkerchief here is that it should mean nothing, that it should indicate only its indicative function, as making out the one who carries it, and tries to transfer it, as 'it'. In a sense, 'it' is a perfect designation of the handkerchief itself; not a particular object, but just an object, which by that token becomes the object, the definite article, the article that defines. But, like the 'the', or the 'it', its essence is to be transferable, to be carried across.

Handkerchiefs are always being left, lent, borrowed, or purloined. Remember the scene, played out in many films. She has started to emit incipient sniffs or full-blown banshee howls, and he produces from his top pocket a voluminous handkerchief, with which she sobbingly blots. Both of them know the ceremonial exchange, which needs no comment or explanation, without knowing how they know it. She weeps, he staunches, it is the way. The handkerchief is a kind of gratuity, a kindness, a charity, a mercy. George Herbert draws on a well-established Christian tradition when he writes in 'The Dawning', 'with his burial-linen dry thine eyes: / Christ left his grave-clothes, that we might, when grief / Draws tears, or blood, not want an handkerchief'.[1]

Handkerchiefs are stolen, as well as lent or given, this being much more common in the past when handkerchiefs were more costly. Not surprisingly, the language of crime is rich with terms for handkerchiefs. A 1699 Canting Dictionary gives 'to cloy the clout' or 'nap the wiper', both meaning to steal the handkerchief, with a 'wiper-drawer' being a handkerchief stealer; a 'queere-clout' is a coarse or ordinary handkerchief, not worth the napping; while a 'rum-clout' is a valuable cambric or holland handkerchief.[2]

The tragedy of Shakespeare's *Othello* turns famously around the disastrous errancy of a strawberry-spotted handkerchief. It is given by Othello to Desdemona, dropped by her, picked up by Emilia, who passes it on to her villainous husband, Iago, who then throws it into the chamber of Cassio, who arranges to have it copied, which Othello discovers and takes as proof of Desdemona's infidelity, with murderous consequences. Thomas Rymer found it ridiculous to build an entire tragedy around such an item of lost linen:

> So much ado, so much stress, so much passion and repetition about an Handkerchief! Why was not this call'd the *Tragedy of the Handkerchief*? We have heard of *Fortunatus his Purse*, and of the *Invisible Cloak*, long ago worn thread bare, and stow'd up in the Wardrobe of obsolete Romances: one might

think, that were a fitter place for this Handkerchief, than that it, at this time of day, be worn on the Stage, to raise every where all this clutter and turmoil.

He even mockingly proposed a happier and more uplifting ending, in which Desdemona's handkerchief would have got tangled up among the bedsheets rather than dropped and stolen, so that 'this Night that she lay in her wedding sheets, the *Fairey* Napkin (whilst *Othello* was stifling her) might have started up to disarm his fury, and stop his ungracious mouth'.[3]

Handkerchiefs can survive ordeals as well as helping us through them. We had a dachshund called Ringo when I was little. It was savagely, pathologically ravenous, and would gag down handkerchiefs whole, like a python. I have always imagined that the digestive system of a dog ought to be able to do away with anything, but Ringo's spurned these handkerchiefs. He would strive to evacuate them on our front lawn, back legs spread wide, front legs scrabbling. Sooner or later, my mother would have to pinch between thumb and forefinger the little tip of white that tongued from his behind (she was a nurse and so we regarded her as uniquely qualified for this duty), and, in front of passers-by by the front gate, tug out from the straining creature the miraculously uncorrupted fabric, now neatly furled into a cylinder, like a sort of extruded intestine, or the twisted sheet one might use to climb out of a burning building, or the string of streamers a conjuror might produce. Just before the clownish moment of separation, as Ringo went one way, and Vivien Connor the other, the handkerchief would seem as long as the animal itself, as though the sausage dog had been transformed into a kind of hanky dispenser.

The handkerchief is a paradoxical object because it is both intimate (it used often to be referred to as a pocket handkerchief) and yet also detachable. It is like a piece of magic skin, which is impregnated with the physical being of its owner (sometimes literally, as in the case of a handkerchief infused with perfume and personal odour), and yet can all too easily be separated from its source. Detached, it remains a part of that from which it has come apart. In this sense, like many another magical object, it is a conjuring cousin-once-removed of the hand itself. Following the execution of Charles I, who had revived the practice of the King's Touch to cure scrofula, stories circulated of magical cures being effected by application of a handkerchief nobly stained with his blood.[4] Curative powers were similarly ascribed to the handkerchief of St Peter. But handkerchiefs, like the gloves with which they are often associated, can also be carriers of mischief. It is alleged that in the early 1960s, the CIA attempted to dispose of Abdul Karim Kassem, the leader of Iraq, by sending him a monogrammed, poisoned handkerchief.[5]

Handkerchiefs are ambiguous – both ordinary and everyday, and yet also special, precious. They are coverings, veils, but also wipers away of pollution. There is always something improvisational or magically metamorphic about a handkerchief, which is always being deployed for other purposes. Handkerchiefs seem never quite to know their place. The kerchief is from Old French *cuevre-chief*, combining *couvrir* to cover and *chief, chef,* itself a modification of *capo*, or *caput*, the head. So a neckerchief, or a handkerchief, is an odd thing – a head-covering for the hand, or for the neck. Since the chief purpose of a kerchief is to cover the head, somebody with a handkerchief knotted on their head is a primitivist, but nowadays will strike us as having perverted the handkerchief's function as a sopper-up or stauncher.

The versatility of the handkerchief is attested to by the many different names for it in different European languages: in Italian a *fazzoletto*, or facecloth; in Dutch, it is a *snotlap*; in German a *Taschentuch* (pocket-cloth); handkerchiefs carried by the lower orders in England were known as *mokadors*, *mokedores*, *muckenders* or *muckiters*.

Handkerchiefs come from nowhere, they are required just to be there already, when required, as though they were woven from our need for them. This is why they are a staple of the conjuror, perhaps. Magical things happen under the spread handkerchief – watches can be smashed to smithereens, and then restored whole, doves can be hatched, birdcages full of chirpers can be vaporised. And, of course, handkerchiefs themselves have a tendency to multiply, as though from some imaginary umbilicus through which the world can be threaded, transformed into an endless line of further handkerchiefs.

This is why it seems so apt for the phrase 'hanky-panky' to have transferred during the early twentieth century from the language of magic to that of sex. Hanky-panky is perhaps a variant of the game 'handy dandy', a guessing game in which an object is transferred between two hands, sometimes with the accompaniment of the phrase 'handy dandy, prickly prandy which hand will you have'.[6] Like 'hocus-pocus', it was perhaps a deliberately empty or distractingly meaningless bit of phonetic flutter, which mimes the action of waving a handkerchief to distract the eye while the conjuror's other hand effects the trick unseen. Hanky-panky now evokes the magical indeterminacy of sexual relations, which conceal the most serious desire and intent under the cover of infantile mischief or harmless naughtiness.

The handkerchief has also shown a tendency to oscillate during its history between a noble and a debased condition. Handkerchiefs had ceremonial functions in the classical world – the *mappa*, or napkin, was dropped to mark the start of the Roman games, for example. These then passed across into various ceremonial cloths employed in the Christian Church. Secular handkerchiefs began to appear in Europe from about the thirteenth-century onwards. They certainly do seem to have had hygienic uses in principle – one of the earliest names for them in French inventories is 'pleuvoirs', or weeping-cloths. The first mention of a handkerchief in English is during the reign of Richard II, in a reference in around 1384 to little pieces of material that were carried by the king 'pro naso suo purgando', in order to wipe his nose. Indeed, a case has been made by some historians that Richard II is to be regarded as the inventor of the pocket handkerchief in the modern sense.[7] But handkerchiefs spread out during the sixteenth and seventeenth centuries, first through the court, then through the aristocracy, primarily as decorative and luxury items. Handkerchiefs were carried or worn, rather than being kept in a pocket for use. Along with fans and gloves, handkerchiefs formed part of an elaborately formalised language of posture and gesture (being incorporated into dance movements, for example). It was not until during the eighteenth century, with the spread of the handkerchief among the middle classes, that it could become a 'pocket handkerchief'.[8]

And yet, all this time, handkerchiefs had a growing centrality in what the German sociologist Norbert Elias describes as the 'civilizing process', in which the pressure grew to separate civilised manners from obviously biological processes and actions.[9] Nose-blowing seems to have had a particular, and surely understandable, importance in this process. From the early sixteenth century onwards, writers on manners and civility such as Erasmus began urging the use of personal handkerchiefs for emunctory purposes instead of sleeves (or tablecloths). Not only were handkerchiefs recommended, the specific ways of using them began to be prescribed. Giovanni della Casa urged

> And when thou hast blowne thy nose, use not to open thy handkercheif, to glare uppon thy snot, as if yu hadst pearles and Rubies fallen from thy braynes: for these be slovenly parts, ynough to cause men, not so much not to love us, as if they did love us, to unlove us againe.[10]

Handkerchiefs have an odd relation to time. Knots are tied in handkerchiefs as reminders, as interruptions or punctuations in the fabric of time. To wave or drop the handkerchief is traditionally to set the game or race in motion. Michel Serres uses a spread-out handkerchief to image the two conditions of history, one flat, in which different historical moments and periods are distributed in a kind of map, with stable and consistent relations of proximity and distance – there the death of Socrates and the Norman conquest, and over here the Industrial Revolution and the flu epidemic of 1918. But crumple up the handkerchief, and what ensues? All of a sudden things that should be far apart are cheek by jowl and nose to toe. Serres proposes that we might think of history just as much in terms of the unexpected adjacencies of this kind of crumpled time as in the more traditional terms of the line.[11] Spanish people say 'El mundo es un pañuelo' – the world is a handkerchief, a small place;

Serres's little emblem flips this sentiment from space to time. In this respect, the handkerchief is an allegory of itself, as well as of many other kinds of magical object, for it is itself both ancient and contemporary. It is a veritable *mappa mundi*, the animate diagram of its own unfoldings.

8

Keys

I am holding a key level in my hand. It is a Yale key, to the jagged profile of which Craig Raine once memorably compared a dog's grin.[1] But is also a mountain-ridge, a city skyline, a lightning bolt, a seismograph, a dying man's scribble, a spreading fracture, a furious arpeggio, a fever chart, a stock-price graph. Strange that something that seems so random, something so like the result of an accidental shearing off, should guard such power of access, should be the guarantee of such trust and security. Like gramophone records, keys seem as though they should be legible. Like all intricate patternings, they seem to be full of import, to have something to say to us, if only it could be made out. In the boxy cuneiform of the classical mortise, the nervous cursive of the Yale, keys are all a kind of writing in iron. But we would need some kind of master key to decipher the code that they are written in. Keys seem to ask the question, to what kind of question might I be the answer?

It is one of the many convolutions of the relations of locks and keys that locks – which in French are called 'serrures' and in German are called 'Schlüssels', both meaning closings or contractions – should necessarily include openings as an essential part of their operations (indeed, the English word 'lock' derives from words meaning a gap, opening or lack). A lock can also provide a loophole, and the keyhole is the fatal flaw in the room of one's own, the chink that can let in slivers of chill air, evil emanations and the eyebeams of the peeper (Satan was thought to be able to insinuate himself through the keyhole of a locked room, sometimes in the form of a fly).

The human imagination is drawn to the keyhole and we are all lookers-in on things. In the comics I read as a child, peepers at keyholes invariably ended up with a telltale blazon in the classic ankh-shape of a keyhole sootily stamped over one eye. The folklore figure of the keyhole peeper, Peeping Tom, Peter Pry, or, in the female version developed for the British comic *Dandy*, Keyhole Kate, is an ancient one: 'Friend of the keyhole and the crack, / That lets thee pry within and pore, / Thy very nose betrays the knack – / Upturn'd through kissing with the door'.[2] Jean-Paul Sartre curiously offers in the picture of a peeper at a keyhole a summary of a kind of being lost in looking. In one sense, the peeper is appropriative. The whole world is shrunk down to what can be sucked in through the greedy pinhole of the eye. But at the same time, the peeper is also shrivelled down to his or her act of looking, becoming 'a pure mode of losing myself in the world, of causing myself to be drunk in by things as ink is by a blotter'. The exhilaration of peeping consists in the fact that it slims us down to a kind of ecstatic vacuity. It is perhaps kneeling at the keyhole that, for Sartre, we become that nothingness we essentially are: 'not only am I unable to know myself, but my very being escapes – though I am that very escape from my being – and I am absolutely nothing'.[3] There are many folk beliefs and rituals that impart special knowledge to the squinter at a gap or keyhole; whoever can be seen at the altar when one looks through a church keyhole on New Year's Eve is doomed to die the following year, while maidens can predict their own marriages if they peek through a keyhole into a barnyard and see a cock and a hen together.[4]

Human beings have lived for centuries with carceral dreams and nightmares that centre on the actions of locking and unlocking. Keys represent power, nowhere more emphatically than in the papal emblem of the crossed gold and silver keys, which are the symbol of the power of the Church, both in heaven and in earth, in fulfilment of Christ's promise to St Peter in Matthew 16:19: 'And I will give to you the keys of the kingdom of heaven. And whatsoever you shall bind upon earth, it shall be bound also in heaven: and whatsoever you shall loose on earth, it shall be loosed also in heaven'. These keys therefore signify not just the dual capacity to lock and unlock, they also signify the sympathetic interlocking at a distance of heaven and earth.

The problem with making out the meaning of keys is precisely that they are so locked into their signification. Keys are so over-taken by the ideas of which they are the vehicles, the meanings to which they are, well, the keys, that we read straight through them, leaving their material features unregistered. Keys are at once hard-ware and software, stuff and sign, matter and idea, sensible and intelligible. The older keys are, the larger they are; ceremonial keys used to be borne upon a steward's shoulder, like a mace. Keys have lost much of this trusty, rusting pomposity. They have thinned and dwindled to the condition of cards, especially in hotels (although in less well-equipped hotels you may still find yourself issued with a key attached to an enormous weight or placard, to make it less likely that you will lose or appropriate it, I suppose). Or they have lost all materiality, becoming abstract ciphers or the keywords we now use to unlock knowledge.

Like many other riddling objects and magical machines – screws, plugs, levers – keys have the power of conversion. There is more than one way to get through a locked door; one can employ the 'king's keys', the crowbars and hammers used by the authorities to force entry to locked premises. Or one can turn a key in the lock. On the one side, brute force, with much expenditure of energy; on the other, artifice and cunning, with a very large return from a very small kinetic force. Like the lever, the key can literally make light of things (especially since the key card must often also be inserted into a slot to make the lights work), yielding up a gratuitous something for nothing amid the remorseless double-entry world of *quid pro quo*.

But, whether slimline or heavy-duty, keys seem always to have had magical purport and propensities, as, for example, in the many variants of divination by Key and Bible. Reginald Scot provides one of the earliest accounts of this in his *Discoverie of Witchcraft* of 1584. If a theft is suspected, the names of suspected thieves are put into the hollow shank of a key, which is then placed against Psalm 49. The Psalm is then read, and when the words 'If thou savest a thief thou didst consent unto him' are reached, the book and key will fall, and whatever name is left in the key will be that of the malefactor.[5]

Men's keys are, for the most part, kept hidden from view, but close at hand, in a pocket, that strange, ruminative dream-cavity that is neither quite inside nor outside of myself, that my hand occupies and explores as my tongue probes my gums and teeth. Like coins, keys provide a kind of rosary resource in times of stress or repose.

Keys embody what might be called the logic of the fit. According to this logic, there is nothing in the universe that can be wholly solitary or singleton, for everything has its couple or complementary other half. For every left hand a right, for every nut a bolt, for every foot a slipper, for every lock a key. Keys signify the two-sidedness, the handedness, the handy-dandiness of nature. It seems entirely right that viruses and antibodies should use something that is very close to a lock-and-key arrangement to bind on to their hosts and enemies, so that having immunity to a disease is literally like having a set of keys to certain antigens. In many species, the male organ of intromission has developed into fantastically elaborate patterns, none, apparently, more so than the European rabbit flea, which has a baroque arrangement of hooks, spirals and barbs, perhaps in order to ensure, Prince Charming-style, that it mates only with a compatible female. I remember the lovely shiver of corporeal consent I experienced when I first heard a painter explain that he would need to roughen the surface of a window frame to give the new coat of paint a key; it instantly told me everything I needed to know, and somehow already did, about the microphysics of surfaces. Lucretius' explication in *De Rerum Natura* of the atomic theories of Democritus and Epicurus depends upon a similar intuition about the links between micromorphology and outward form. Suave and agreeable things, like honey or milk, are so, he tells us, because the atoms of which they are made are round and smooth, whereas sharp or bitter things are made up of atoms with jutting or jagged edges. Similarly, he goes on, hard things, like diamonds, or the bolt of a door, are so because they 'must be composed of deeply indented and hooked atoms and held firm by their intertangling branches'.[6] This being Lucretius, he finds a way to make the very form of his verse mime this intricate interlocking – the literal translation 'there must be hooks hooking between them' letting slip the tight internal rhyming of 'hamatis inter sese esse necesset' (II.445). But what is rhyme anyway but the system of locks and bolts that hold songs and poems together?

I have always loved stories of escape, especially when they involve the outwitting of lock-and-key confinements. I often return in my mind to a ruse I first read about in a comic as a boy, feeling sure that there will one day be an occasion for me to use it. If you are locked in a room where the key has been left in the door on the other side, slide a sheet of newspaper under the door, poke the key out on to the newspaper and pull it carefully back on to your side. Keys are bilateral. They lock things in place, keeping them apart; but they also unlock and unleash. The key thus embodies the two primary principles of alchemy, of *solve et coagula*, dissolution and thickening.[7] In China, a key may be given to an only son to lock him into life and in Germany a key in a cradle kept the child from being stolen; but keys may also be slipped under the pillow of a dying child to ease its passage into death.[8]

Keys are proverbially cold. At the beginning of Shakespeare's *Richard III*, Lady Anne greets the corpse of her father-in-law Henry VI as the 'Poor key-cold figure of a holy king'.[9] A cold key dropped down the neck is supposed to cure a nosebleed, presumably because the shock of the cold is presumed to seal or anneal the ruptured blood vessels that are causing the flow. So why, I always wondered, should the key not be applied to the nose itself? This seems to imply a secret set of correspondences between different parts of the body, such that a lock applied in one part will close off an aperture in another. The cold key here is a thermodynamic engine, as it is elsewhere a mechanical one.

There is something strangely cryptic and forlorn about a single key. It seems to be in the nature of keys to cluster. There is comfort and copiousness in the very word we use for this aggregation: 'bunch'. The bunch of keys has served for centuries as the sign of a wife's local dominion over the house. In medieval France, a woman who was left without sufficient provision to pay her deceased husband's debts could eschew responsibility for them by throwing into his grave the bunch of keys she carried at her girdle. A Victorian housekeeper would wear a bunch of keys at her waist. The young Freud counted among the domestic delights that lay before him and his fiancée Martha Bernays 'a large bunch of keys which must rattle noisily'.[10]

The threat that can accrue to a key that is separated from its bunch is indicated by the Grimms' story of Bluebeard. Bluebeard's wife is given a bunch of keys that will give her the run of the castle, but is forbidden to use the smallest of the keys. When curiosity gets the better of her, she discovers the room full of the mangled remains of her husband's former wives. In her terror, she drops the key on to the bloodstained floor and, despite all her scrubbing, is unable to clean away the blood from it. When Bluebeard returns, the bloody key tells him that she has disobeyed him.

Bunches of keys offer a bouquet of possibilities for playful fidgets. If I am in a leisurely and expansive frame of mind, I will lay out my keys in my right hand, splayed like a corona, or a second, metal hand, and poke through them with my left forefinger, for the key I want. When I am standing at my door, unwilling to relinquish the clump of carrier bags that I have in my left hand, I must perform this trick one-handed. I thrust my right forefinger through the hole of the keyring and, using this as a hanger, I proceed to flip the keys one by one with my thumb up and over my anchor finger, in a motion like that of tossing coins.

A large part of the allure and enigma of keys rests in their versatile sound-profile. One could imagine an entire carillon of keys, running down all the way from portentous clang to elfin tinkle. In his poem 'Among Those Killed in the Dawn Raid Was a Man Aged a Hundred' Dylan Thomas contrives to make the blowing of keys from their locks an improbable kind of bell-ringing celebration: 'The locks yawned loose and a blast blew them wide /… When all the keys shot from the locks, and rang'.[11] But keys, like their musical cousins, are sociable noise-makers. The surf crash of a bunch of keys tossed on to a table has a triumphant, cashbag kind of opulence, combined with the thrilling, exhilarating suggestion of a smashed window. By contrast, the probing scurry and crunch of a key in a lock can express a world of hesitation and menace. The turnkey's 'clink' (which may relate to Dutch *klink* and German *Klinke*, the latch of a door, as well as recording a sound) gave its name to one of the most dismal prisons in medieval Southwark, and is still a generic word for jail among Londoners.

But the real secret of the key is the ever-present possibility that it can be lost. I am a pickpocket's ideal target, as I perform every few seconds the secular rite of signation (self-crossing) that involves patting the three pockets where my phone, keys, wallet and comb are kept. The sense of security I get from the keys in my pocket is completely inseparable from the repeatedly awakened panic that they may be lost. Here, the massiness of keys is indispensable to their meaning. The sickening clot of apprehension that forms in the bottom of my stomach when I pat my keys-pocket and find, not the clumpy cluster that should be there, but mere, appalling flatness, matches exactly, as key to lock, the keys' absconded mass.

As well as the danger of losing keys, there are dangers to which keys expose us. In the Gex region of France, a young girl would never move a bunch of keys on a Wednesday, for fear of losing her wits.[12] The speaker of a nineteenth-century comic poem is driven to such desperation by his search for his wife's lost keys that he starts to turn into an effigy of what he has lost:

> Search! Search! Search!
>   Till the eyes grow heavy and dim.
> Drawer and pocket and shelf,
>   Shelf and pocket and drawer.
> Till I dream that I am a key myself,
>   And wonder what lock I am for.
>
> But why do I talk of despair!
>   That phantom of grisly bone,
> With reddened eye and ruffled hair,
>   It seems so like my own.[13]

If keys are easily lost then so, surprisingly, are locks. Most houses have a collection of keys that no longer fit any known locks. There is perhaps nothing so orphaned, clueless and yet also so full of quizzical possibility as a key separated from its lock. The collectors of antique keys seem bent on redeeming them by clustering them together, ordering them by style and make, as though to rescue them from their refugee condition. But nothing can help the sense of amputation that lockless keys give, even when congregated with their likes. They suggest a powerful, uneasy asymmetry, like a collection of left-handed gloves.

Keys form much more useful assemblages when they are gathered together into what we call keyboards, whether they are musical or computational. The key that so resembles a kind of illegible writing is thus made into a means for writing production. Every now and then a thread will be started on a computer users' forum by somebody asking how best to clean their keyboard. No such discussion can go for long before somebody reports the fact that keyboards have more bacteria on them per square centimetre than a toilet seat.

Writers on the arrival of the keyboard are pretty unanimous in their view that the keyboard is a kind of disciplining or constraining of the body. For such writers, computation is amputation. But the striking thing about typing and our different kind of address to different kinds of keyboard and array is how tenderly personal our relationship to it is. Far from being a sign of our disembodied condition in the world of modern communications, the keyboard is a witness to the persistence and participation of the body in such actions at a distance. The traces of this intimacy can be seen in erosion and deposition, the compatibility and compassion of things. As I look down at the keyboard I am using to type this, belonging to a laptop computer that is only a few months old, I can see already the distinguishing marks that make it as close a fit to me as my shoes, with their distinctive patterns of scuffing and wearing down.

Viewed in a slanting light, there is a damp-looking shiny patch in the middle of the touch-pad and on the right-hand side of the space bar. Elsewhere across the keyboard there are other small handholds indicating where I have been a frequent visitor, as well as spots that appear almost immaculate – I don't even know what the F3 key does, and am too nervous to try it now. My keyboard is my handiwork – it is beginning to form a dactylographic offprint of my manual gait, as I variously skate, peck and blunder over the land-scape of letter-keys spread before me. I imagine that, viewed under a powerful microscope, each key would display a different portrait of overlaid fingerprints (not necessarily from the same finger, as I am an inexpert and improvisatory typist) all slightly out of phase with each other, reflecting the different angles of attack I employ to hit individual keys. Taken all together, my keyboard is surely a single, infinitely sensitive key to the work in progress made by my operations upon it.

9

Knots

 **Knots have two** strongly contrasting aspects that are, as we might say, knottily intertwined. First of all, and perhaps primarily, the knot is the embodiment of constancy or coherence, of that which holds or binds together. It is easy to imagine the origins of beliefs in the magical efficacy of tying and interlacing, given the obvious yet still always miraculous strength and efficacy of knots, in sailing, engineering, weaving and mechanical operations of all kinds. Knots are often mnemonic, the taking up of a stitch in time as a stay against forgetfulness. Even more than speech, accounting and mathematical procedures seem to depend upon knots, most systematically in the *quipu* system, in which knots are made in a series of coloured cords to record information. The system flourished under the Incas and remained in use, or at least intelligible, in parts of Peru until late into the twentieth century. The *quipu* seems to have functioned as a method of

mathematical notation and perhaps as a calculation aid too, and some scholars suspect that the knots also encoded much more complex forms of narrative and historical record and thus constituted something like a writing system.[1] Maritime knots are a measure of time projected into space; speed would be measured by counting the number of knots in a rope paid out from the back of the ship in the time it took for the sand to run through a half-minute glass. Nowadays, the number of knots at which a ship is travelling is the number of nautical miles (minutes of the earth's longitude at the equator) that a ship is covering per hour.

The primary virtue of the knot is in seeming to hold up, to hold out against, time. There are many examples of knots being used as amulets, to preserve health or fortune, one of the most notable being the *tyet*, or knot of Isis, a three-looped knot which seems to suggest a human figure, and the related ideograph of the *ankh*. The Egyptian Hedjhotep was the god both of weaving and amulets, and knotted cords were known as 'Anubis threads' , since Anubis presided over the practice of wrapping the corpse in mummification, the ultimate form of bodily preservation against the dissolutions of time.[2] Indeed, the use of knots in spells may well condition the sense of the magical power of writing itself, which is concentrated in its own loopings, and power to turn time back on itself. The knot embodies the most extreme magic of all, namely reversibility, in a temporal world in which in reality nothing ever remains in its place or comes back. In a knot, the top and the bottom, the left and the right turn into each other.

Knots were thought to encourage the knitting together of wounds. Pliny the Elder reported on the wonderful healing powers in particular of the Hercules knot or 'nodus Herculanus', an expression used by classical authors to refer to a riddle or logical puzzle that was extremely hard to construe. I give his description in Philémon Holland's translation:

> As for greene wounds, it is wonderfull how soon they will be healed, in case they be bound up and tied with a Hercules knot [marginal note: Wherein no ends are to be seene, they are so close couched, & therefore hardly to be unloosed]: and verily it is thought, that to knit our girdles which we weare about us every day with such a knot, hath a great vertue in it, by reason that Hercules first devised the same.[3]

Knots also feature in magical remedies where their function is to ease or to diffuse pain – for example, in the use of a snakeskin knotted nine times and worn for nine days round the wrist as a charm against rheumatism.[4] Presumably in this case the function of the knot is to confirm that the power of the remedy continues to be held and concentrated in the curative or prophylactic object, even as it is given out as a kind of unloosing.

Knottings and crossings feature frequently in heraldry, and survive in badges or emblems of affiliation of many kinds, of companies, guilds and clubs, as well as in ceremonial ties, garters and cravats, all of which signify the close-knit continuity and the unity-in-multitude of the association. Such images or sigla, which are often worn on the body, might actually double and fold back into it certain magical forms of the body itself. It has been suggested, for example, that the use of knot amulets in Egyptian magic had a primary reference to the vertebra, as suggested by the ideograph *ts*, which signifies both knot and vertebra, since the vertebrae may be thought of as 'a series of bony ligatures, links, or connected segments comprising the spine, that is, they are the series of "knots" that tie the whole skeleton together'.[5]

Knots have a particular centrality in Judaism because of the *tallith*, the prayer shawl, with its eight tassels, each tied with five knots; this adds up to 13, which, added in turn to the number 600, the numerical value in the *gematria* system of the word *tzitzit* (the collective term for the eight tassels), makes 613, the total number of precepts in the Torah.[6] Thus, whelmed in the *tallith*, the body of the observant Jew is bound into the entire body of the Law. But, if the law is bound up in the form of a knot, there is also a law that is binding on knots themselves. The Babylonian Talmud contains a chapter explaining in what circumstances one may tie or untie a knot on the Sabbath – according to Rabbi Meir, '[o]ne does not become culpable for any knots that can be untied with one hand' – as though what were proscribed were the mimetic knotting of the body involved in the tying of knots.[7]

The power of the knot to countermand time can also take malign forms. J. G. Frazer records that a parliament in Bordeaux sentenced someone to be burned alive for bringing systematic ruin to a whole family by means of magical knotted cords.[8] There is a tradition in some commentaries on the Koran that the prophet Mohammed was bewitched by a Jewish magician, who tied nine knots in a cord and hid it in a well. It was only when the Angel Gabriel revealed the whereabouts of the cord, and incantations were said over it to cause the knots to loosen, that the Prophet recovered from his sickness.

The ambivalence of the knot is nowhere more manifest than in the sphere of love and sexual association. Tying the knot is, of course, a powerful image and metaphorical guarantee of fidelity in love, as is witnessed in the many forms of the true lover's knot, often woven from hair, which lovers have given to each other as pledges, and in traditions of the intertwining of the red rose and briar springing from the graves of sweethearts, as in the folk song *Barbara Allen*. In marriage, the *not* of the 'virgin knot' is undone by the 'knotting' that, in popular parlance, once meant copulation, even as marriage itself can be thought of as a less congenial kind of bondage, as in the popular description of a wedding as 'tying a knot with the tongue that cannot be untied with the teeth'.[9] For this reason, knots have a central place in many marriage and betrothal ceremonies.

But knots, which ought to turn the couple inwards on themselves, can also come between them when others intervene, inhibiting their congress, or preventing its issue. Touching the bridegroom with a handkerchief and then tying a knot in it is one way to go about preventing consummation. Understood in this way, the knot does not join, but blocks up. Witch's knots were believed to be used for the purpose of creating impotence or barrenness. James I singles out as examples of 'such kinde of Charmes as commonlie dafte wives uses' the practice of 'staying maried folkes, to have naturallie adoe with other, (by knitting so manie knottes upon a poynt at the time of their mariage)'.[10] In the ballad *Willie's Lady* (Child ballad no. 6), a jealous mother casts a spell on her son's new bride that prevents her not from conceiving but, even more cruelly, from giving birth to her child. The spell is eventually discovered when her son fashions a simulacral child out of a loaf of wax and invites the mother to the christening. When he hears her raging 'Who was it who undid the nine witch-knots / Woven in among this lady's locks? / And who was it who took out the combs of care / Braided in amongst this lady's hair?' he immediately performs the required operations, and his wife is given her deliverance.[11]

Just as wedding ceremonies in different cultures often require the couple to leave buttons undone and shoes unlaced, there are also many beliefs and practices involving the systematic unloosing of knots or the prohibition of braiding, or crossing of legs, at a time of childbirth. These anxieties and prophylactic practices extend to other times of life passage as well, including death. Frazer provides the rationale for this in homeopathic principles: 'Whether you cross threads in tying a knot, or only cross your legs in sitting at your ease, you are equally, on the principles of homeopathic magic, crossing or thwarting the free course of things, and your action cannot but check or impede whatever may be going forward in your neighbourhood'.[12] The principle that like affects like, no matter what spatial distance may intervene between the objects bound together, has an odd parallel in physics in the principle of 'quantum entanglement', or the theory that two particles may be able to affect each other even though they are separated. The knot implicates the far in the near and the near in the far.

A knot is the magical image of time turned upon itself. There is an important difference between a knot and a loop, bow or circle. For these latter merely mark or suspend time, open up a nook or epoch in time, a passage of time in which time can appear not to pass. But a knot does more than merely remit the onward pressure of time, for it also turns it against or back into itself. A loop slackens the tension of ongoing time, but a knot makes that tension strive against itself, so that, the more one pulls on the two sides of a knot, the tighter it gets, time coagulating into space and space becoming ever more charged with time.

Yet, for this reason, knots can also keep time open, by storing up possibility. In this respect, knots hold time proleptically in store, or hold it back from itself. An interesting knot practice is recorded among the Southern African Nandi people; a traveller starting a journey will make a knot in some grass by the side of the road, in the hope thereby of preventing those he is going to visit from having their meal before he arrives, or at least of ensuring that there will be food left over.[13] Probably this is why the tying together of the loose ends at the end of a narrative is also called a *dénouement*, or unknotting – for once the knot has been slackened, nothing more can happen. A knot is a prevarication, a provocation and a promise of more to come. John Scheffer reported in his *History of Lapland* that Finnish sorcerers 'sell winds to those Merchants that traffic with them, when they are at any time detained by a contrary one. The manner is thus, they deliver a small rope with three knots upon it, with this caution, that when they loose the first, they shall have a good wind, if the second a stronger, if the third, such a storm will arise, that they can neither see how to direct the ship, and avoid rocks, or so much as stand upon the decks, or handle the tackling'.[14] Knots could also be used for divination purposes, presumably on the principle that they knitted together the present and the future that were normally held apart from each other. One such procedure was recorded in the early nineteenth century: 'Whenever I go to lye in a strange bed, I always tye my Garter nine times round the bed-post, and knit nine Knots in it, and say to myself: "This Knot I knit, this Knot I tye, to see my Love as he goes by, in his apparel'd array, as he walks in every day"'.[15] In Papua New Guinea, knot magic is used to conduct transactions with one's own death. A grieving relative who wishes to have their death hastened will tie some knots in a leaf and throw it to the *yambukei* egret, hoping that it will fly to the land of the dead, who will come in a canoe in the appointed number of days to fetch the spirit of the supplicant.[16]

The two meanings wound up in knots, the conservation from time, and the constraining of time, do not neutrally cohabit. Rather, they initiate and engender each other. The knot concentrates a power of unloosing, disperses a power of retention. The knot is a figure for the logical difficulty of paradox not because it simply makes the paradoxical relation plain or lays it open to view, but because it is itself paradoxical and self-confuting. A knot is a figure that offers to help us grasp all at once the idea of something that can neither quite be pulled apart or pull itself together. It is implicated in what it signifies.

The knot is the image of life itself, with man as the anastomosis of spirit and body, in which, as in John Donne's 'The Ecstasy', is 'knit / That subtle knot, which makes us man'.[17] The dissolution of death is the untying of that knot. Pressing the snake to her bosom, Cleopatra demands 'With thy sharp teeth this knot intrinsicate / Of life at once untie'. But knots also stand for the obstructing effect of complication, and therefore for secrecy, conspiracy and a kind of perverse proliferation. Indeed, the motivation to Cleopatra to seize the writhing asp is that she thinks that if Octavia 'first meet the curled Antony / He'll make demand of her, and spend that kiss / Which is my heaven to have', where curling may refer both to Antony's coiffure and his coiling betrayal.[18] Discovering the plot against him, Ford in *The Merry Wives of Windsor* howls 'there's a knot, a ging, a pack, a conspiracy against me'.[19] Conspiracies are presumably thought of as knots because they are paradoxically fissiparous fusings, conjunctive dissensions, with no basis but their own self-generated solidarity.

The modern mathematics of knots arises from a similarly self-propagating convolution of something from nothing. Watching his colleague P. G. Tait perform experiments with a device for producing smoke rings, William Thomson proposed in 1867 that the basic constituents of matter might be nothing more than vortices or convolutions in the ether, that ultra-attenuated medium of universal transmission in which occult and scientific traditions come together.[20] Though it has a distant descendant in modern string theory, the theory of 'vortex-atoms' and 'ether-knots' was soon abandoned, but not before it had set in train the still prospering form of mathematics known as knot theory. In a sense, the power of the knot is precisely that it images the empty self-relation of that which comes into being in turning or reflecting on itself, and is thus twin to the self-conjuring *cogito*. A knot is not so much a magical object in itself, as a magical form, or the precipitate of a magical practice. It is a way of doing magic with, and imparting magical possibility to, more mundane objects – laces, ribbons, hankies, wires and hair. Indeed, the definition of a magical object I offered earlier, as something that helps us credit our own powers to invest objects with magical powers, has something characteristically involuted and knotty about it. Perhaps all magical objects are knottings together of objects and the subjects that conjure with them.

10

Newspaper

 **Consider the difference** between these two questions: 'Have you seen the paper?' and 'Have you got some paper?' In the first case, the paper in question is clearly a specific kind of paper, namely a newspaper. What is more, the definite article strongly signals that it is today's newspaper that is being referred to, or at least a newspaper regarded as still in some way current – the first daily newspaper in Britain, which appeared in 1702, was in fact called the *Daily Courant*.[1] The indefiniteness of 'some paper', on the other hand, indicates that any paper will do – the construction here is known as a partitive, because it suggests that a part of some amorphous mass or collection is being indicated. The dropping of the definite article, the 'the', means that the newspaper is itself no longer a definite article, an entity, a specific, bounded thing, distinguished clearly from other things, but has been transformed into a general stuff. This is indicated strongly by the fact that one of

the most obvious uses for newspaper is precisely as stuffing, simply occupying space – as in the newspaper that plumps out the arms and legs of the effigies of Guy Fawkes on November 5th. If there is one thing as humble as being a waste of space, it is amounting to no more than the space you fill. Such sad stuff, newspaper, sad with the sadness of the lost, the missed, the all but all over.

In the one case, what matters about the paper is precisely not its matter, but the signs, the news, it carries. Indeed, when it is 'the paper', the very awareness of the thinness and disposability of the paper on which it is printed draws attention away from it to the information it carries, indicating that it is a matter that does not matter. As soon as it is no longer 'the newspaper' but 'newspaper', or just 'paper', it is no longer reading matter, and the signs it bears become, as we say, immaterial. So, actually, the very word *newspaper* is as metaphorically two-sided as a piece of paper: on one side is paper, with news printed on it, on the other is news, once new, but which has deteriorated into the condition of waste paper. Newspapers are an emblem of the impermanence of writing, the subordination of writing to time. Time pulps the differentiality of newspapers – pro-government, anti-government, Establishment, sporting, samizdat, quality, tabloid – into pure indifference. It strips away definite and indefinite articles from newspapers; they cease to be 'a newspaper', or even 'the newspaper' – as in, 'I read an article in the newspaper' – and become just stuff.

Michel Serres has pointed out that philosophers traditionally distinguish two orders of thing in the universe, which he calls the hard and the soft.[2] Hard things are physical – stone, water, glass, metal, flesh, and so on. Soft things are not soft in the way in which blancmange or a baby's bottom are soft, but in the sense that they are the form or the conception rather than the substance of a thing. So, on this definition, matter is hard, information is soft. This is an ancient distinction, one that Aristotle drew on when he proposed that, in conception, women provided the matter of the foetus, while men injected the formative principle, but it is alive and well in the distinction between software and hardware. More than any other matter, paper moves and mediates between these orders of the hard and the soft. The oddity lies of course in using the word 'soft' – which names a physical quality – to signify that which has no specifically physical qualities. Ideas do not in fact have material density and texture. Physically, a newspaper may seem to move from a relatively hard condition, dry, crisply folded, bulky, with a very specific kind of shape and heft to it, to a soft one, crumpled, torn, damp, blurred. In terms of the distinction I am borrowing here, though, the newspaper actually moves from the soft to the hard, from information to matter, from idea to stuff.

I have been suggesting in this book that many material things are liable to embody some kind of untimeliness, some form or other of anachronistic hiccup or syncopation. But newspaper is distinctive because it is temporised matter through and through. Of no other form of matter is it so true that the simple passage of time seems to change its meaning and its substance so swiftly and drastically. The word 'ephemera', which is used to designate transient or temporary pieces of paper, like playbills, trade cards, and wrapping, seems to have a special link with newspapers, deriving as it does from Greek *epi-*, of, concerning, and *-hemera*, a day. Like the fabled day-fly, the newspaper lives for only one day. 'Where could we live but days?' as Philip Larkin wonders.[3] But how could there have been days in quite the sense in which we understand them, before there were newspapers to mark and measure their coming and going? Newspapers are not only contemporary and therefore temporary, they are also metachronic, in that they keep the very beat of time. Newspapers are not just daily, they make for the occurrence of days, turning days into dates. Indeed, for this very reason, newspapers can be used as timepieces, as when victims of kidnappings are photographed holding up a newspaper as proof that they are still alive, or were at the time the photograph was taken. We establish the same link between days and dates when we collect the newspapers published on our birthdays. I've often thought it would be quite as emblematic, if admittedly a bit lugubrious, to collect all the newspapers published on the date of a person's demise.

Ours is a house of the book as the Jews are said to be the people of the book. Books are never discarded, and never abused in our house; a dropped or creased book is a painful disgrace, and even detective stories and embossed-cover soft porn are shelved with care and respect. For most people, newspapers are the opposite of books. Even the people who hoard newspapers, and I do know some, cannot be intending to keep them for ever, but just until they get round to reading them. At that point, they will have been used up. Of course, the keeping of newspaper cuttings has been established almost as long as newspapers themselves, but the album, which tries to keep the newspapers new, to provide a reservoir against time, only succeeds in slowing it down. To keep a book is to preserve it; to keep a newspaper is simply to delay its reversion to matter.

The extreme vulnerability to being used up makes the newness of newspapers especially poignant and precious. Men seem to need to be the first in any household to broach a newspaper and many of the men I know, so neglectful of so much, seem to harbour tender and pious feelings for newspapers, especially in relation to their foldings. For such men, and for me among them, I confess, just running your eyes over a newspaper is enough to transform it into something used up, or on the way to being so. In reading a newspaper, you cannot keep your act of reading immune from the effects of your bodily attentions. Newspapers are entropic allegories. There is nothing you can do to a newspaper that does not start and participate in this deterioriation. But a newly delivered folded newspaper is as pristine as a newly bathed baby. I have never been surprised to read that the inside of a fresh newspaper can be used as a sterile covering *in extremis*. When one uses a ball of newspaper to impart a diamond glitter to cleaned windows, one is demonstrating the power of the newspaper to spread its renovating quality to other objects.

Newspaper performs humble offices, once its job of carrying news is over and it has itself grown old. But, because of its quick and conspicuous ageing, paper is not merely humble, it is also humiliated and to some degree humiliating. This is what gives the jeer in the chorus of the Rolling Stones's 1967 song 'Yesterday's Papers' its vicious sting: 'Who wants yesterday's papers? / Who wants yesterday's girl? / Who wants yesterday's papers? / Nobody in the world.' There is something sordid about newspapers and so it is not for nothing that newspapers are called 'rags'. The speed of the transformation of 'the newspaper' into newspaper makes the pain and pathos of its degradation unignorable. And this prospect in turn is built into the experience of turning over a brand-new newspaper. The freshly baked neatness and crispness of a newspaper has belatedness and beggarliness stored up in it.

Newspapers may represent the sacramental transfiguration of matter into sign, but the reading of a newspaper is more intimately involved with physical process than the reading of any other kind of text. The newspaper only has a weak kind of directionality. The reading space of the newspaper is much more diversified, animated by the order and quality of its reading, than the uniform space of a book page. The eye is not enjoined to move steadily through the newspaper's text, but skips, scoots, circles and skids fly-wise around the page. As Nicholson Baker has put it, newspapers 'have a visual exorbitance, a horizon-usurping presence'.[4] Many readers of newspapers do not even read sequentially through its pages in numerical order, but turn to the sport, the crossword, or the letters page in a personal order of preference. You read a newspaper as you eat a meal – a slice of chicken or a fardel of green beans here, a dab of sauce there – not as you tell a joke or sing a song.

The newspaper may seem anomalous if our model for reading is the book. But the newspaper is perhaps paradigmatic of all reading, in the sense that it actualises the affordances or existential opportunities of paper, in allowing us to scan, jump and collate across documents, rather than having to burrow through them.[5] In this sense, at least, reading a text electronically is a much more primitive and one-dimensional operation than reading a newspaper – as the phrase 'scrolling through a text' aptly suggests.

Electronic texts also flatten out the difference between sizes and formats of newspapers, in which class differences are also so strikingly encoded. A broadsheet newspaper is defined by the Oxford English Dictionary as 'considered to contain serious, in depth journalism'. Somewhat counter-intuitively, the broadsheet, the more intellectual newspaper format, involves much more obvious and

energetic bodily skill and commitment than tabloid and other formats. This probably involves the application of a sumptuary principle, in that having the leisure to expend so much energy on such a
simple task may act as a display of status. It suggests that one is
accustomed to spreading out one's newspaper on a reading desk, or
taking up one's station behind it in a leather armchair in one's club.
But broadsheet readers have to develop considerable manipulation
skills nevertheless. One must learn how to read with arms spread in
the posture assumed by visionaries at the moment of their apotheosis, moving one's whole head and neck over the expanse of the
double page like an animal nuzzling around a nosebag. The mari-
ner's tact is required to keep a broadsheet readably aslant to the
wind when reading outdoors. And, most virtuoso of all, there is the
trick of reducing the mainsail folio of the newspaper into quarto- or
octavo-sized slabs for reading in crowded trains and aircraft seats,
combined with the matchless accomplishment of turning over
whole pages, quartile by quartile, in their correct order.

The newspaper is nearly as adaptable as the cigarette as a pos-
tural and gestural accessory. It can be rolled, made into a fan,
submitted to all kinds of complex origami. It can be made into
hats and boats (hats which are boats and boats which are hats).
My Scouse father assured me that, on the terraces at Liverpool's
Anfield football stadium, before the advent of all-seater stadiums,
the *Liverpool Echo* was formed into funnels into which the straining bladders of spectators could be discreetly vented. Groundlings
seated next to the pitch at the bottom of the cataract were well-
advised to bring waterproof footwear to the match.

As it passes from news to paper, from sign to stuff, the newspaper moves from the condition of the flat, the charisma of which we

have already encountered in the form of the card, to the voluminous. If there is something magical in this capacity to expand into three dimensions, it must also be seen as part of the degradation to which newspapers are so uniquely heir. Newspapers decline into senescence by rising into the condition of a body. The crease or wrinkle in the immaculate flatness of a newspaper is the first intimation of this decay from the flat into the fat.

One of the defining physical features of the new newspaper is its desiccation and consequent absorbency. As it ages, newspaper becomes moist – humid as well as humiliated. The butler who would iron the newspaper was doing so for two reasons, to flatten out any creases, but also to dry out the ink, so that it did not come off on the master's hands or gloves. Flatness and dryness are equivalent signs of the abstract and the inorganic. To fall away from the condition of a sign is also to fall into the condition of the organic. T. S. Eliot evokes this possibility in his 'Preludes': 'And now a gusty shower wraps / The grimy scraps / Of withered leaves across your feet / And newpapers from vacant lots'.[6] Those 'withered leaves' may equally be of cabbages and newspapers. Becoming more bodily itself, newspaper, reduced to an indefinite article, is adapted to bodily uses, as for example in the account given by Samuel Beckett's tramp Molloy:

> in winter, under my greatcoat, I wrapped myself in swathes of newspaper, and did not shed them until the earth awoke, for good, in April. The Times Literary Supplement was admirably adapted to this purpose, of a never failing toughness and impermeability. Even farts made no impression on it.[7]

Wrapping oneself in sheets of newspaper is a neat reminiscence, and reversal, of an earlier epoch in the history of paper. In the absence of papyrus reeds, which had died out in Egypt in the tenth century, or the paper mulberry tree, which was used to make paper in China, where it originated, rags, from worn-out clothing and other textiles, were the principal raw material for papermaking in Europe until the eighteenth century.[8]

There are other physical functions into which newspaper is drawn in its degraded latenesses. One of them is eating. In Britain, during the twentieth century, fish and chips have traditionally been wrapped in newspaper, which performed the office both of keeping the meal warm, and of soaking up the grease. There is an even closer association with eating in the use of paper as a construction material, in the form of what has been known in English since the mid-eighteenth century as papier mâché. This expression literally means 'chewed-up paper' and human beings who have played host to mice and other rodent guests over the centuries know how glad they are to find paper which can be shredded finely to make nesting material. There is, alas, no direct etymological link between the words 'pap' and 'paper', but the affinity of sound suggests that we have a strong apprehension of what might be made of masticated newspaper. Indeed, the idea of using wood as a source for making paper was first suggested to the naturalist René Réaumur in 1719 when he saw wasps making their nests from chewed-up fibres.[9] One of the delightful aspects of this pulping of newspaper is that it recapitulates the beginnings of the material, which is formed from sheets made of similarly pulped cellulose fibres from herbs and trees.

Newspapers have two destinies. In one, they are transfigured through and into fire. My first and most lasting acquaintance with the architectural powers of newspaper came from watching my father light a fire. This was an exquisite and loving art. Everything depended upon the latticework of sticks and lumps of coal, built up in such a way as both to provide a mass of fuel and enough in the way of cavities and channels to allow the flames through. The essential mediator between mass and vacancy was newspaper, scrunched into slightly springy balls and rolled into toffee-like twists. Once this edifice had been raised, with the same kind of care to the ordering of actions and the disposition of elements as that enjoyed by the first four chapters of Leviticus, which specify the ways in which one should prepare burnt offerings of bullocks, goats and turtledoves to provide 'a sweet savour unto the Lord' (Leviticus 1:13), my father would lean back in his chair, light up a cigarette and nonchalantly, and if possible without even a glance, toss the match into the fire, which would instantly catch and spread. The essential feature of the construction was the bolus of newspaper balls, which, flaring and blackening quickly, would provide first of all an immediate source of heat to begin to ignite the wood, and then, as they burned away, create a vacuum into which new draughts of air would be sucked, so that the coal could begin to bake red. When I saw space rockets ascending, discarding their used-up stages as they went, I recognised the logic of their design instantly.

Only occasionally were there failures, which could usually be blamed upon the quality of the newspaper (for example, when the damp *Daily Mail* had been delivered to us instead of the cooperatively combustible *Daily Mirror*). But newspaper provided the remedy for these abortions too, for a sheet of newspaper could be placed across the front of the fireplace to encourage the short-winded fire to suck in air from underneath. When as an earnest adolescent I began to read Vladimir Nabokov in search of the art and intellectuality that would secure my passage out of the world of council houses and coal fires, part of me nevertheless had to acknowledge the strong communication between the arts of the word and the arts of the hand to be found in passages like this one, describing Nabokov's application of the same technique to a reluctant fire as a student in Cambridge in the 1920s:

> So I would heap on more coals and help revive the flames by spreading a sheet of the London *Times* over the smoking black jaws of the fireplace, thus screening completely its open recess. A humming noise would start behind the taut paper, which would acquire the smoothness of drumskin and the beauty of luminous parchment. Presently, as the hum turned into a roar, an orange-colored spot would appear in the middle of the sheet, and whatever patch of print happened to be there (for example, 'The League does not command a guinea or a gun,' or '… the revenges that Nemesis has had upon Allied hesitation and indecision in Eastern and Central Europe…') stood out with ominous clarity – until suddenly the orange spot burst. Then the flaming sheet, with the whirr of a liberated phoenix, would fly up the chimney to join the stars.[10]

The other destiny of newspaper is slower and more human than phoenix-like; it is to decay into a mulch, reverting to humus. The implied alimentariness of chewed-up paper points to the most insistent and inescapable aspect of the corporeality of newspapers. As the definitional waste product, newspaper is closely associated with our own excremental issues. The history of the use of paper for bottom-wiping is somewhat obscure. Undoubtedly, it has been used on occasion since early times, though the fact that paper has been until relatively recently an expensive commodity probably discouraged this practice until the age of mass printing made disposable publications common, along with the practice of hanging printed sheets in the lavatory for the purpose of wiping. The first proprietary lavatory paper was J. C. Gayetty's Medicated Paper for the Water Closet, which went on sale in 1857. It made much of the fact that the printer's ink in newspapers, along with traces of bleaches such as vitriol, lime and potash, was likely to cause or aggravate piles, which were, by contrast, eased by the 'soothing medications' in Gayetty's product.[11]

But this history also reminds us of the solidarity between edification and defecation, so masterfully invoked by James Joyce's description of Leopold Bloom reading a romantic story in a magazine in his outdoor lavatory: 'Quietly he read, restraining himself, the first column and, yielding but resisting, began the second. Midway, his last resistance yielding, he allowed his bowels to ease themselves quietly as they read, reading still patiently that slight constipation of yesterday quite gone'.[12] Everything is there: the reciprocity of intellectual intake and bodily output, the matching of the columns of print to Bloom's alimentary column, the musical synchronising of plotting and plopping. My first girlfriend, now, unsurprisingly, a distinguished Professor of English, used to take Anglo-Saxon verbs to cram on the loo. The newspaper often sits between these two extremes, poised, or rather forming a passage, between the empyrean and the underworld. Newspapers become the past because they are so involved in every form of passing.

11

Pills

 **I am not a very habitual pill-popper**, my intake being limited to the occasional paracetamol and an even more occasional course of antibiotics. But, rare recourse though they may be, pills are nevertheless as common and habitual an accessory for me as for anybody else. My briefcase is almost certain to contain a couple of headache pills twisted in silver foil, the bathroom cabinet is crowded with pill bottles, packets and sachets, and there is a large tupperware container in our kitchen that is jammed full of medicaments for two decades' worth of chronic though oddly non-recurring ailments from earache to allergy.

I am, however, an expert swallower of pills, and have never been able to understand why anybody could need water to assist this operation. I have never yet encountered a pill that I could not poise at the back of my tongue and tip back into my gullet in a single gulp. In the comics I used to read as a child, sufferers from streaming colds or headaches induced by falling anvils would often be presented with enormous 'horse pills', the size of snowballs, but they would hold no terrors for me.

There is, of course, an enormous range of medicinal forms and objects – powders, poultices, drops, draughts, infusions, oils, ointments, syrups, tinctures, elixirs, lozenges, pessaries, syringes – all of which are saturated by specific and different kinds of magical feeling. Some of them, like 'tincture' and 'elixir', have alchemical provenance. What characterises the pill is its freedom from what ancient philosophers called 'accidents', that is, features of taste, smell and texture. The glutinousness of cough mixture is a sample and a promise of the soothing effect it will have on your throat. The adhesiveness of a sticking plaster, along with the little pad of healing power islanded amid the stickiness, clearly announces the sealing and supporting and impregnating functions it will perform. The hypodermic needle, all glinting rapidity, point and precision, sharply instantiates its own fearless ethic of going straight to the heart of the trouble. But the pill keeps the secret of its operation hidden, giving no image or intimation in its physical form of the kind of work it will do or the kind of relief it may offer. This, of course, is a kind of magic in itself. Call it a kind of white magic or magic of the neutral, that comes precisely from the fact that the pill is outwardly without qualities. This feature is played on in a satirical description by 'Felix Folio' in 1858 of a Manchester quack's wares, which included 'Female Pills': 'the pills, which were contained in an old tea caddy without lid, were, I suppose, the "females," but, from their external appearance, I should not be able to assign any sex to them'.[1] This is why the pill appears to be so sleekly, unfussily modern.

Though usually to be found in multiples, the pill is essentially aloof and solitary, this perhaps being the reason why contraceptive pills are still known in the form of an honorific singular – 'The Pill'.

Although pills have been manufactured for centuries, most purveyors of pharmaceutical substances have preferred to make use of the symbolism and ritual action involved in the application of different kinds of substances to the body, in contrast to the relatively neutral act of swallowing a pill. Of the more than 1500 recipes in the Hippocratic Corpus, a collection of ancient Greek medical texts, only two are for pills, as compared with 77 ointments, 92 fumigant mixtures, 200 enemas and more than 400 pessary recipes.[2] Pills and pastilles still accounted for only about ten per cent of the medicines manufactured by charlatans in early modern Italy.[3] One important influence on the increasing popularity of the pill was the growing consumerism of medicine during the eighteenth century, during which, as Roy Porter observes, the emphasis shifted from laborious regimens of diet and lifestyle, requiring extensive self-management or expensive medical oversight, to 'the investment of greater faith in the power of the pill – healing power thus becoming crystallized, through some magical alchemy, into tangible commodities'. Indeed, as Porter observes, an analogy seems to have been established between pills and money itself, that similarly all-purpose commodity – quack medicines were very commonly sold at precisely a penny a pill, in shilling or two-shilling packs of twelve or twenty-four.[4] The pill also seems to be an important part of the slow dissolving of the bond between the physician or healer and the patient, who could now begin to self-administer. This has important implications in non-Western contexts, where pills have played an important part in changing traditional relationships between patients and healers.[5]

The primacy of the pill is also the result of the move which took place from the end of the nineteenth century onwards from bespoke products, made up in earlier times by apothecaries and pharmacists, and usually as oral or topical liquids (liniments, embrocations, etc), to pre-packaged products, supplied by pharmaceutical companies. In 1900, sixty per cent of all the prescriptions supplied by a particular South London shop were for various kinds of liquids, with only ten per cent being for solid-dose forms (mostly tablets); by 1980, seventy per cent of the prescriptions were for solid-dose medicines, with only seven per cent being for elixirs or syrups that required any kind of making up.[6] Not that the magical ritual has been entirely abandoned; when a customer goes into a pharmacy to ask for a prescription medicine, the pharmacist will retreat to an inner sanctum to make it up, as though to perform some special mystery of concoction, even if it may only involve counting out a seven-day course of amoxycillin.

The most important and representative modern pill is the aspirin, which was first marketed by Bayer in 1899. The aspirin seemed to be able to treat almost everything, and, though marketed in different forms, its versatility seems to make the white pill its essential form. This in itself has seemed sinister to some. Morris A. Bealle, in a tirade against the American pharmaceutical industry, put aspirin at the centre of a legalised 'dope racket', arguing that '[t]hese dangerous little white pills cover up (but do not cure) headaches, toothache, neuritis, lumbago, sciatica, nervousness and colds … in covering up the pains it gives the victim a false sense that everything is all right'. Bealle went even further, claiming that aspirin causes kidney damage (it can), and that it dangerously dulled perception (unlikely): 'Aspirin doesn't cure anything. It dulls the central nervous system and makes an unthinking person think it has done him (or her) good. When you take an Aspirin, it is ingested into the blood stream and goes thru 56,000 miles of blood vessels. It saturates and partially deadens more than a billion miles of nerves'. He even thought that the indiscriminate use of aspirin would encourage reckless driving.[7]

The neutrality and universality of the pill have also made it attractive to quacks and medical fraudsters. One of the most successful purveyors of patent medicine in the nineteenth century was James Morison, who believed that bad blood was the cause of all illness, which could therefore in every case be cured by application of vegetable laxatives. He marketed his vegetable purges, containing things like aloes, rhubarb and myrrh (so they were going to work), as 'Morison's Universal Pills', which were available in two versions, no. 1, and the stronger no. 2. This hint of carefully graduated dosage is the more risible given that Morison recommended unrestrained use of the pills – the more the better.[8] Satirical prints poked fun at Morison's immoderate claims, and his encouragement of heavy and prolonged use of his pills, showing grass, carrots and cabbages sprouting from the skin of users, a man claiming that the pills have helped his amputated legs grow back, and, in a lithograph of about 1835, a shopkeeper assuring a black customer that 'about two thousand boxes more will without doubt render you as white as a lily'.[9] Many drugs, especially in tablet form, are similarly credited with almost universal powers in some non-Western contexts.[10]

The point of the pill is that, in principle, a precise and predetermined dose can be delivered. But this mathematisation of the medicine cannot prevent overdose. Indeed, it seems to have made it more likely, for exact calibration also allowed for inflation, in every sense

– inflated claims, and immoderate consumption of pills in huge quantities, like the man who was reported to have ingested 226,934 pills between 1794 and 1816 – though even odder than the compulsion to swallow so many pills is the impulse to keep a tally.[11] The compulsion to overdose is also made clear in the patter of a nineteenth-century pill-monger. A man buying 'a family case of pills' from a patent medicine shop is directed to take 'two of number twelve', but inverts the instructions:

> The consequence was, that he very soon had to visit the rear of the premises, and to repeat the journey many times, with very short intermissions. The poor fellow was seen when making his twelfth journey (every shot took effect it appears), and not making his appearance for some hours, his friends sought for him, but, shocking to relate, so effectually had the medicine done its work, that the unfortunate fellow's body *had completely dissolved!* Yes, my good friends, the pills had actually *annihilated him*; and the dreadful fact would never have been discovered, only he happened to be a member of the Society of Friends, and *his hat having an expansive brim, had caught and remained across the aperture through which his body had melted!*[12]

The pills acquired by the dissolving Quaker were clearly laxative, and pills seem to have had a particular use in inducing just such unmentionable functions. Carter's Little Liver Pills were marketed successfully for many years on this basis, while 'female pills', like Hooper's Female Pills, Widow Welch's Female Pills, Fuller's Benedictine Pills and the Golden Pills of Life and Beauty, which offered relief for a number of female complaints, but especially various kinds of 'obstruction', were often discreetly being touted as inducers of abortion.[13] One nineteenth-century advertisement for a 'Wonderful Female Pill' promised that it would 'strengthen, regulate, and purify the system, and give a lively complexion to the palest countenances', but made its real purpose clear in the warning it darkly appended: 'Please take Notice: – These Pills should not be used by ladies who are expecting to become mothers'.[14]

The potent neutrality of the pill has, however, often been resisted. Pills were often coated in gold or silver during the eighteenth century, presumably in order to signal more manifestly the sovereign virtues they possessed. Studies of the placebo effect have often indicated that the efficacy of a drug given in tablet form can be materially affected by its shape, texture and colour. An early study in 1970 showed that the colour of pills taken for depression and anxiety subtly but measurably changed the response of patients to them. Patients were given tablets for anxiety that all contained the same dose of oxazepam, a relative of diazepam (Valium), but coloured differently: red, yellow and green. Green tablets proved to be significantly more effective at relieving anxiety states, especially, for some reason, phobic anxiety, where the green tablets were twice as effective as red or yellow. On the other hand, depressive symptoms seemed to respond better to yellow tablets.[15] Another study of patient preferences showed that the ideal form of a tablet was small, round and white; if the tablet had to be bigger, the preferred format was oblong or oval.[16] And a study in Poland showed that, for Polish women at least, a spherical pill has a more powerful effect than a flat tablet (men showed no such preference), and that big white and small red placebo pills performed better than small white and big red pills containing actual medicine.[17] Others have claimed that blue and green pills have a depressant effect, while red pills act as stimulants, making blue the default colour for sleeping pills.

I can remember being taken aback the first time a doctor advised me to moderate the dose of something I was taking by splitting the pill in half. It seemed to me then, as now, bizarrely unlikely that the therapeutic material could really be uniformly distributed through the material of the pill in the way this implied. I stubbornly continue to imagine the quiddity of the pill inaccessibly inhabiting its tiny, potent core. This, I think, is because the pill appears itself so like a concentrated bead of puissance. If the draught or mixture speaks of a process of manufacture characterised by cunning compounding, the pill advertises itself as the outcome of a compression, which forces in its virtue and locks it in place. I know all about slow release in the gut and so on, but for me, nothwithstanding, the power of the pill, once ingested, is to be imagined as explosive. For this reason, I avoid crunching or masticating a pill; it must be gulped down whole, lest its powerful internal exuberance be dissipated too early amid the teeth and gums. Hence, perhaps, the explosive associations of the pillbox, of popping pills and 'dropping' tabs of acid (like bombs, I suppose). The encapsulated power of the pill is as nothing compared with the dream-power of the idea of encapsulation itself, the black box, the white pill: it is the general force of singularity, with the poetry of multiple meanings.

12

Pins

 **Pins belong to the great** and diverse universe of fastenings, the thesaurus of contrivances that human beings use to latch, loop and lock things together, and themselves together with them. Fastenings instance and embody the capacity and the need to form conjunctures, associations and adjacencies. They effect anagrammatic rearrangements of the things of the world – hooking up hems, attaching badges and emblems to clothing. They collect the world – from *col-ligere*, to bind or gather together, a word that shares an etymological root with the word 'religion', along with words like 'ligament', 'allegiance', 'obligation' and 'liability'. The safety pin, in particular, '[l]igature of infancy, healing engine of emergency, base and mainstay of our civilization', closing together on itself as it brings other things close to each other, may be regarded as the meta-pin, or king-pin of pinioning.[1]

But of all the range of fastenings, subtly suggestive as they always are of security and surprise, pins are the most ambivalent, because the most impermanent. Pins have about them always something of the adapted, the temporary or the makeshift. A skirt or a trouser leg that is pinned up is done so as a place-holder or preparation for the more permanent suture of stitching. A popular song of 1908 devoted improbably to the subject of pins observes that, useful as they are for so many other things (cockle-eating, lock-picking), hairpins are strikingly ill-adapted for their nominal office:

> There's only one thing it won't do, 'tis useless for the
>   hair!…
> Girls, don't use it for the hair, you're silly if you do,
> It's always falling out, and then your hair is falling too,
> To keep your hair on use a net, or stick it on with glue,
> It's a sin – to trust a pin – Hair-pin.[2]

It is for this reason that, though they are closely associated, pins and needles, needles and pins, are also in fact nearly opposites. Where a needle effects a magical merging or weaving together of two substances, a pin adjoins without joining; the coiled or collateral substances remain alongside each other, face to face, spliced yet separate, and so easily able to come apart again. There is always a certain looseness, a play of possibility, in pinning. The reason why you shouldn't pin your hopes on something is that pinning is contingent rather than permanent. This is perhaps why, though one can readily be pinned down – by enemy fire, or by swarming Lilliputians – pinning seems more properly associated with pinning *up*, in a way that emphasises that which is held up against the countervailing pull of gravity. The tense excitement of piled hair is precisely the sense it seems to give that pulling out a single pin may bring it cascading down, in voluptuous sweet catastrophe.

Pins are puny, minor, inconsiderable things, which makes them apt figures of negligibility itself. To say that one would do something 'for two pins' is to indicate that very little inducement indeed would be needed; 'I don't give a single pin what the world thinks of me' sings the Saucy Sailor in the folk song of that name. It is rare for a currency to have a coin small enough to purchase a single pin, even though pins, like buttons, can themselves form miniature kinds of currency. It is because of this minuteness that pins are also so fugitive, so easy to drop, spill, forget and mislay. A writer in *Punch* reflected in 1842 that, if only all the 20 million pins that were produced a day and mysteriously disappeared could be recovered, it would be enough to build a huge iron 'Victoria's Pin' to rival Cleopatra's Needle at Alexandria.[3]

Pins have not always been so negligible. Though pins of bone and wood have been in use for thousands of years to join clothing and to hold hair in place, metal pins were much harder to manufacture and consequently were prized as luxuries until the seventeenth century. Nevertheless, there was great demand for them, especially during the fourteenth century in which elaborate headdress, such as coifs, veils and wimples, required a great deal of pinning, together and up. Pins were extensively used in women's dress well into the seventeenth century, after men's clothing had started to be held together by buttons and buckles. During the fourteenth century, pins were in short enough supply and expensive enough – you could buy a sheep for what 500 pins cost – that they were allowed to be put on open sale on only two days of the year, January 1st and 2nd.[4] 'Pin-money' was the allowance made to women to buy luxurious items of this kind – there was actually a special tax levied in France to keep the Queen in pins – and the term only gradually dwindled down to its current meaning of an extra, rather inconsiderable bit of income on the side.[5] By the seventeenth century, pins had become common enough for them to stand as the measure of the almost nothing. A broadside ballad from 1660 includes the verse:

> On Nothing I think, on Nothing I Write,
> 'Tis Nothing I Covet, yet Nothing I slight,
> And I care not a Pin, if I get Nothing by't[6]

William Cowper formed this poetic riddle around the enigma of a pin:

> A needle small, as small can be,
> In bulk and use, surpasses me,
>   Nor is my purchase dear;
> For little, and almost for nought,
>   As many of my kind are bought
>   As days are in the year.[7]

Pins are incidental objects, but, for this very reason, can also be associated with precision and acuity. Innumerable and negligible as units, they can nevertheless sometimes be used to count or measure. 'A pin a day is a groat a year' goes an English proverb.[8] The incremental power of pins to go from small to large is shown in the famous use of pin-making by economist Adam Smith at the beginning of his *Wealth of Nations* to illustrate the advantages of the division of labour into specialised tasks, calculating that a factory employing ten men in this way could expect to produce 48,000 pins a day:

Each person, therefore, making a tenth part of forty-eight thousand pins, might be considered as making four thousand eight hundred pins in a day. But if they had all wrought separately and independently, and without any of them having been educated to this peculiar business, they certainly could not each of them have made twenty, perhaps not one pin in a day; that is, certainly, not the two hundred and fortieth, perhaps not the four thousand eight hundredth part of what they are at present capable of performing, in consequence of a proper division and combination of their different operations.[9]

Google maps reassure us that they are giving us the precise location that we seek by an icon of a large-headed pin marking the spot. The pin is identified with the abstract, absolute exactitude of the single point, which is why a pin approximates in imagination to an idea of something like an atom or elementary particle of space. Hence the expression 'counting angels upon a pinhead', used to ridicule absurdly minute and hair-splitting speculations. The phrase may well have its origin in Thomas Aquinas's objections to those who 'crediderunt quod angelus non posset esse nisi in loco punctali' – who believe that an angel is not able to exist except in a punctual position.[10] Aquinas is in fact making the point that angels do not occupy physical space, but this somehow got turned, in anti-Catholic polemic, into the idea that he was absurdly preoccupied by the effort to bring together the spiritual and the physical in the locus of the pinhead. Thereafter, the pinhead has become the measure of a magical packing or concentration of infinite riches in a little room – such as, for example, the inscription by Israeli scientists at the University of Haifa using a laser beam of the entire 300,000-word text of the Hebrew Bible on to a silicon surface measuring 0.01 inch square, which was inevitably compared in news reports to the head of a pin.[11] Unconsidered, inconsiderable, scarcely a thing at all, a pin is often nevertheless the very thing, the thing itself, both negligible and necessary. This may be in part why we have got into the habit of referring tautologically to PIN-numbers (a PIN is already a Personal Identification Number). Your PIN is a number that pins you down, ensuring that you stick to yourself.

There is danger in pins, too – the voodoo doll or the witch's waxen image stuck with pins is both an image of cruelty, and the proof that an image is all one needs for cruelty's work. In Europe, pins are strongly associated with the work of witches. A seventeenth-century pamphlet tells the story of an old woman who begged from a maidservant called Elizabeth Burgiss a pin to fasten her neckcloth. Several days later, the maid began to complain of sharp pricking pains. A hand thrust down the back of her dress disclosed 'a great piece of Clay as full of Pins as it could well be'. This was thrown into the fire, but the pains recurred. This time, investigation produced 'a piece of Clay as thick of Thorns as the other of Pins'.[12] Joan Butts, the old woman thought to be responsible, was tried as a witch the following year, but acquitted. The vomiting up of prodigious numbers of pins was often held to be indisputable proof of the effects of sorcery or witchcraft.[13]

Magic is not always required to make for the malice of pins. Pulling out the pin is the prelude to the grenade's detonation. The hatpin has frequently been turned to aggressive or defensive uses, and Hamlet observes that a man 'might his quietus make / With a bare bodkin', a bodkin being a lady's hairpin.[14] Indeed, Herodotus tells a story of a man returning to Athens as the sole survivor of a disastrous military expedition against Aegina in the sixth century. The enraged widows of the slaughtered men formed a circle round him, demanding to know where their husbands were and jabbing him with their clothing pins until he died. Herodotus says that the women were punished by being forced to change to a style of dress that did not employ pins, while the Aeginetans celebrated by passing a law requiring their women to use pins that were half as long again.[15] The passage of the expression 'being pinned down' from domestic to military contexts testifies to the power of the pin to suggest uncomfortable or painful arrest. T. S. Eliot's Prufrock evokes the pain of being socially locked in position through the metaphor of the mounted butterfly – 'when I am formulated, sprawling on a pin / When I am pinned and wriggling on the wall / How should I begin'.[16]

Even when not deployed directly by witches, pins have often been thought unlucky. A nineteenth-century witness described the precautions taken by the captain of a fishing ship when an apple pie was brought on board wrapped in a napkin secured with pins: 'One man held it, and the captain cautiously took out each pin, and with arm extended to the uttermost, carefully dropped them over the counter into the sea to drown … The captain then slowly, seriously, and solemnly assured me that pins were spiteful witches, and ought never to be brought on board a vessel'.[17] It used also to be thought to be bad luck for a bride to go to her wedding with a pin left in her dress, the idea here perhaps being that the sharpness of the pin is dangerously reversible. Leopold Bloom adduces a different reason in Joyce's *Ulysses*, in which he reflects 'Women won't pick up pins. Say it cuts lo' (he means love).[18] The two sides of the pin are expressed aptly in its two ends, the head and the point; a condition sometimes attaching to the picked-up pin is that its point should not be towards you – to pick up such a pin is in fact to risk pricking up misfortune. This logic may in turn underlie the superstition that one should never lend a pin; in the North of England, the request to borrow a pin may once have been met with the reply 'You can take one, but I haven't given it to you'.[19]

And yet there is also magical virtue in pins. There are many evidences of the belief that 'pins and needles are a protection against the malice of the servants of Satan'.[20] They can be used to guard against witches, for example through the preparation of 'witch-bottles', containing nails and pins, or by sticking pins in one's doorpost.[21] There is a report of a piece of bacon porcupined with pins being hung in a chimney to put witches off making their entry that way.[22] Just as witches were thought to inflict tortures on their victims with pins, so they were themselves cruelly probed with pins to find the telltale *stigmata diaboli*, marks or spots of insensibility.[23] In Iceland, pins driven into the feet of corpses discouraged the deceased from walking after their interment.[24] If it is unlucky for a bride to have a pin in her dress, a pin inserted into a gambler's lapel ensures success.[25] Perhaps because they are so easy to lose, and their loss is of so little account, adventitiously found pins are often thought of as lucky: 'See a pin, pick it up, / And all day you'll have good luck. / See a pin let it lay, / And your luck will pass away.' Milliners used to believe that a box of pins dropped signified a rush of sales.[26] On the other hand, a pin can be used to combat loss; if you lose something, then stick a pin into a cushion, with the words 'I pin the devil', and the lost object will quickly come to hand.[27] There is a widespread tradition that pins may be dropped into wells by women to propitiate its resident spirit or the saint associated with it and bring good luck.[28] The fact that sometimes these are crooked pins may also relate to the desire to prevent reversal of fortune, or because there is a special virtue in a pin, that already duplicitous object, which has itself been doubled over in this way.

The doubleness of pins is to the fore in their association with love and sexual relations. Pins are associated with courting, for example in the American folk song that begins 'I'll give to you a paper of pins / For that's the way my love begins', but also with the constraint of marriage: 'Needles and pins! Needles and pins! / When a man's married his trouble begins'.[29] The pleasurable sizzling of incipient sexual attraction can be like pins and needles – but there can be apprehension in this sensation too – 'by the pricking of my thumbs, / Something wicked this way comes'.[30]

Being themselves so easily transferable from place to place and from office to office, pins seem to have the magical power of taking on and transmitting the qualities of other things. There is a tradition that a wart can be cured by touching it with a pin and dropping the pin into a bottle, which is then buried; as the pin rusts, so the wart will shrink. In another version, pins are driven into the warts, then stuck into the bark of an ash-tree.[31] Oh, and be careful never to take into your mouth a pin that has been used in a shroud, for it will rot your teeth.[32]

The pin has a good claim to being thought of as the most trans-formable of objects, making it a kind of 'stem-thing', that is capable of being turned into almost any other thing. Of no object is this more true than the paper clip, which is in essence a bent pin. According to Howard Sufrin, the heir to the Pittsburgh-based paper-clip firm, 'three out of every ten paper clips were lost, and only one in ten was ever used to hold papers together. Other uses included toothpicks; fingernail and ear cleaners; makeshift fasteners for nylons, bras, and blouses; tie clasps; chips in card games; markers in children's games; decorative chains; and weapons'.[33] No object, not even the elastic band, is more allied to active contemplation than the paper clip.

Because pins join things together temporarily, they are themselves mobile and transactive objects, which move between their different contexts like so many of those on which I meditate in this book. Pins of various kinds form connections and passages in machines and constructions. To 'turl at the pin' is to apply oneself to the door handle. Pins are therefore, like coins and other objects that undergo rapid passage, ideal narrative objects – in fact they are something like an image or engine of narrative itself. The narrator of *The History of a Pin* hands over the narrative to her subject with the words 'We shall leave her to tell it in her own way, and in the first person singular, indicative mood, past tense, as every decently grammatical individual, whether pin or person, ought to do'. Here, the pin is slyly affiliated to the 'I' itself, both the fullest expression of subjective experience, and yet also the most elementary, almost accidental stroke of the pen. The story of the pin pins together the great realm of the indiscriminate – two pins being as alike as anything can be, except possibly two peas – and the *hic-et-nunc* particularity of an individual point of view. And yet, as *The History of a Pin* reminds us, 'pins are always ladies'.[34] It has been suggested that '[s]ome ingenious philosopher could write a full tractate on woman in her relation to pins – hairpins, clothes-pins, hatpins, rolling-pins'.[35] In such stories, the pin, like the coin, really has no story of her own; she is at the centre by being always on the fringe of things; she is merely an onlooker, an overhearer, a fellow-traveller, a facilitator, a connector, a compiler, a switchboard operator. She is a lynchpin. Hans Christian Andersen's 'The Darning Needle' tells the story of a proud needle's passage through various stages of decline, from a needle darning fine clothes and shoes, then, after she is broken, a simple pin with an improvised head of sealing wax, then washed away in the gutter, then making a mast for an improvised eggshell boat. Even after being crushed by a wagon, she remains diminished, but irreducible: 'she didn't break, even though a whole cart load had gone over her. She was lying at full length – and there she can stay!'[36] As close as makes almost no difference to nothing, the pin can never quite be brought down to it.

13

Pipes

**Once, after a heavy snowfall**, a damp patch appeared on my ceiling; it spread, swelled and began ominously to weep. When I went into the loft to investigate, it turned out that the heat from the house was melting the foot or so of snow on the roof above it, and the melting water was entering through a single cracked slate, then streaming by capillary action, in a runnel scarcely a bead of water wide, swiftly along the top of a joist all the way to the next room, where, finding no exit, it was pooling around the wick formed by an electric light fitting and forming the swamp in the plaster I had seen from below. I got out on the roof and shovelled, but could make little impression on the snow. As further snow was forecast, it was not going to be possible for me to remove the prodigiously piled and ever-renewing source of the water. My only option was to go with the melting snow's flow and try to encourage it in the idea it already had, so as to channel it away. So

I gathered together all the bits of rubber tubing and plastic pipe I could, including a length of neon light fitting, and joined them together, in a crazy, flimsy chain. I then, with some difficulty, inveigled and finagled the thin thread of water to hop across from its conducive beam into my improvised drain, and drew it some twenty feet across the loft, ensuring that the gradient would dip, slightly, but steadily, to where a hole in the ceiling already existed for a water pipe. I widened this hole to allow a rubber tube through, which I then guided out of the gap at the top of a sash window. In this way, gallons and tons of water were piped into, through, and out of the house. It was, like most such improvised projects, a lesson in moral physics, in how by indirections to find directions out. I had learned good conduct.

The pipe may be thought of as the materialisation of a mathematical vector. The simplest and most primary form of the pipe is the line scooped out by a flow of liquid along a particular track. Gradually, what is first the narrowest of indentations becomes a runnel, and then a gutter, and then a channel. Only a covering is needed to make it into a culvert. There is perhaps a survival of the idea of this primary way of way-making in every pipe: even though most pipes have been made for the express purpose of carrying flows – of water, gas, and other matter – the pipe seems self-made, blindly nosing and boring its way along. The pipe is a magical compromise between visibility and invisibility. Conspicuously, sometimes obscenely visible though they are themselves, pipes nevertheless conduct a secret ministry.

And yet pipes also effect a rationalisation of space; they belong to the human effort to re-sort the world's random assortment of things into more orderly and efficient arrangements. The pipe concentrates and simplifies a ramifying, dilatory and unreliable flow into something express and purposive. The network of pipes, like the network of wires, turns a landscape, with all its jagged accident and lumpy irregularity, into an idea. Where in the past roads would be compelled to cross rivers by means of bridges, it has become common to route whole rivers across roads or railway lines through pipes. As archetypal transports, pipes not only move things from place to place: they change the notion of space itself. They are the sign of our fundamental topophobia, our dissatisfaction with space and with its proximities and distributions. This must go there; that must come over here. No wonder that for decades, the possibility of life on Mars was indicated by the existence of what seemed to be canals. How have humans transformed the world? By pipework: plumbing, drilling and boring, in mountain tunnels, underpasses, submarine passages, in the channels we bore through the air, by the silver tubes we travel through them in.

But piping can never entirely be on the side of the rational. This is largely because pipes borrow from and remind us so intimately of the human body, in which pipes are so messily legion. For hundreds of years, it was assumed that the nerves were hollow pipes through which animal spirits travelled, communicating sensation to the brain and motive impulses leading to movement in the other direction, from the brain to the members. The importance of the many other kinds of pipe, tube and channel in the body was equally not lost on early anatomists and physiologists. The pipe is both the most elementary and the most ramified form of internal communication and connection in the body. Indeed, one view of the human body reduces it in essence to a single tube, which takes in nourishment at one end and expels wastes at the other end. At the core of the human apparatus are the intestines, but perhaps the whole corporeal frame is nothing more than a complication or interruption of this tube. I stand ministering to the radiator with a bleeding key, as, only a couple of centuries ago, a physician might have sought to siphon away bad blood. Even the astronaut floating at the end of his umbilical cord of air and communications reminds us that we come into being at and as extensions of pipes.

Pipes are old-new. They seem increasingly to belong to a hydraulic world in which the most important passages and circulations were of forms of liquid matter – water, petrol, blood, gas – rather than information. The earliest fantasies attaching to electric wires were as kinds of pipes, along which physical materials or qualities might be transmitted. I cannot have been alone in my childish fantasies of smell-o-phones, or phones that could convey sweeties.

I am not sure whether channels, ditches and pipes were first used to carry things to where they were needed, or to carry them away from where they were offensive, but I would bet that the requirements of drainage and disposal came first. Nomadic peoples can move away from their wastes and towards their sources of food; settled peoples must send their wastes away and arrange for their necessities to be conveyed to them. The drain introduces the most striking feature of the pipe, namely its clamorous crypto-vocality. Where water swirls into a waste pipe, it gurgles, as though in surly protest (I have never been able to hear any laughter in the sound of a drain). The gargoyles that adorn the gutters of churches and cathedrals are visualisations, even physiognomies, of these sounds. The very name 'gargoyle' means a gurgler, and is etymologically related to the Gorgon, both of them sharing an origin in the Sanskrit word *garg*, which seems to mean simply to make the sound *garg*, along with the kind of gagging face you pull when you make it. All pipes carry in them the hint and imminence of this kind of guttural utterance. There is a secret correspondence, therefore, between the pipes that exist as conduits of gas and liquid matter and musical pipes, for all of the former can lapse into the latter. The animating principle is usually the commixture of gas and air, as in the bubbling and grating of the straw at the bottom of the milkshake, or the wheeze of the asthmatic trying to get his clogged squeezebox to draw. The Hebrew word *ruagh* (roo-ach), the creative inspiration of air, seems to suggest this in the very rasping of the air against the throat it enjoins. This is not a free but a retarded expression of air, so there is a growling, animal oscillation of flesh in the very articulation of the word for the animating power of spirit. Something is held back in the sound, it is the sound of a reluctance or obstruction, something haunts and corrupts in it.

This poltergeist spite, this creaking heaviness of spirit, always seems to lurk in pipes, especially at their weak points, the bend, in which smell and sediment gather, and the joint, which seeps and leaks. Their misery and menace mature at night, when we can lie in bed and hear them whining and wheezing, hissing and whooshing, banging and knocking. They are a kind of capillary unconscious, the groaning of things under the yoke of their utility, sobbing their glottal stops, coughing and crooning sullen agues and inertias. They sing of catarrh, catastrophe, quarrel, blockage, eddy, doldrum, blowback.

Although in principle pipes can allow passage in two directions, in practice pipes tend to convey their contents only in one direction. This is largely because historically pipes have depended upon atmospheric or gravitational pressure for their motive force. Veins, water mains, gas pipes, beer pumps and alimentary canals are all unidirectional. The word 'catarrh' means 'downflow', from Greek *kata-*, down, and *rhein*, to flow; the uvular rattle of the Greek *rhein* can also be heard purring in the old word *rheum* and in 'diarrhoea', which means a flowing-through. But the sense that pipes are in essence asymmetrical, and flow, like rivers and sewers, in one direction, nudged or tugged by a single gradient, is what lies behind the sense that, when that flow is interrupted or reversed, it creates danger and apprehension. When a pipe rattles violently on the turning off of a tap, the phenomenon is known as 'water hammer': it is caused by the sudden build-up of a pressure and the recoil of a shock wave from the obstruction. The great exception to the rule of unidirectional flow is the human windpipe, which allows for movement in both directions. But the very fact that, below the pharynx, the channel leading from the mouth and nose divides into the trachea and oesophagus means that, at any one time, the flow of air and food has to be carefully regulated, by the operation of the epiglottis, the little lid that closes off access to the trachea when food or drink are being swallowed. The hiccups and spasms that result when this regulation does not work properly are the peril that attends the human pipe. All such thwartings and recoilings in a pipe seem to portend the last guttering crepitus in the throats of the dying.

And yet the very fact that the inexorable one-way flow of the pipe can be slowed or complicated also means that it can enact the pleasurable thickening, suspension or complication of time. Pipes effect and are themselves the effects of the variation of speeds. All things flow, said Heraclitus, but not at the same speed, and not in the same direction. Pipes selectively intensify certain flows, marking and embodying differentials in speed. As rivers and other watercourses, they come about spontaneously as the lines of momentum, the desire of flowing things to evade or overcome the inertia of whatever it is that lies in their way. Currents are the desire of flow to form channels, to groove and striate space. There is in fact no empty undifferentiated space, for all space, whether in the ocean or in the ocean of the seemingly empty air, is bored by channels. Blowpipes, peashooters, rifles, cannons are all accelerators. The music of different kinds of pipe arises from just such regularised constrictions of the column of air.

The human habit of smoking is another example of this kind of finessing of flow. When the first travellers to America in the sixteenth century saw the North American native peoples smoking, it was usually with a pipe (Mayans preferred to roll the tobacco leaves into cigar-like cylinders), and it was pipe smoking that became the preferred mode of tobacco inhalation that spread during the seventeenth century, first across Europe, then into all parts of Asia. It was not until the end of the nineteenth century that the cigar started to become popular in Europe, followed, almost a century later, by the cigarette. The cigarette became associated with the sophistications of modern life and the consumption of mass-produced commodities. The pipe reciprocally became more and more the sign of traditional, rural or indigenous cultures.

Not the least of the fascinations of the pipe used for smoking is that it is an exterior prolongation of the internal breathing apparatus it supplies. One nineteenth-century commentator called the pipe of the Germans 'a natural portion – a part and parcel – of their capilliferous physiognomies'.[1] The same applies to many wind instruments, especially those that seem to mimic the interior convolutions of human pipework, like trumpets, euphoniums and bagpipes. Unlike the cigar or cigarette, which allow immediate and continuous contact with the source of smoke, the pipe is designed to ensure distance, delay and complication. The whole point of the pipe is to permit and promote lingering and procrastination. The cigarette usually comes ready-made, but the pipe must be prepared, sometimes with elaborate ritual. But then the action of smoking the pipe puts the smoker at some kind of remove from the tobacco, which enacts fantasies of filtration and purification. One nineteenth-century pipe enthusiast explains his preference for the simple English clay pipe over Continental designs on the grounds that it yields a purer kind of smoke:

> for what can equal the slender, graceful beauty of the pure white stem, gently curving like a willow-wand in the breeze, with its crimson tip emulating the most brilliant coral. The draught, too, is easy; and the white smoke flows through the tube, like milk and honey unmixed with the dead and disagreeable flavour of tobacco-oil or tar, which the meerschaum and other standard pipes, however carefully cleansed, always retain.[2]

But the point of the smoking pipe is also to effect and participate in a kind of transformation and interfusion. This is emphasised by the fact that smoking pipes are usually made of materials that themselves absorb as well as transmit smoke, often undergoing slow transmutation over time. Gradually the Meerschaum pipe will age and darken as it absorbs the tars of the smoke. The fact that many pipes have been made of clay also suggests this capacity for reciprocal transformation between smoker and implement. Our nineteenth-century celebrant of pipes enjoys the thought that being turned into clay might also mean being 'manipulated by some cunning hand, and moulded into pipes'.[3] The pipe is also a kind of contemplative apparatus, an exteriorisation of cerebral process. The solution of problems by Sherlock Holmes sometimes seems to require something like a dissolution of some considerable portion of the detective himself into hazy smoke, as in this passage from 'The Man With the Twisted Lip':

[H]e constructed a sort of Eastern divan, upon which he perched himself cross-legged, with an ounce of shag tobacco and a box of matches laid out in front of him. In the dim light of the lamp I saw him sitting there, an old briar pipe between his lips, his eyes fixed vacantly upon the corner of the ceiling, the blue smoke curling up from him, silent, motionless, with the light shining upon his strong-set aquiline features. So he sat as I dropped off to sleep, and so he sat when a sudden ejaculation caused me to wake up, and I found the summer sun shining into the apartment. The pipe was still between his lips, the smoke still curled upward, and the room was full of a dense tobacco haze, but nothing remained of the heap of shag which I had seen upon the divan the previous night.[4]

In this story, Holmes has to investigate an opium addict who has gone missing and turns out to be living a double life as a beggar. The popularity of the opium den at the end of the nineteenth century seems to represent the negative apotheosis of the pipe as the sign of decadence and sluggish indolence, the tempting, terrifying opposite of the schedule-driven modern world with its utilitarian flows through pipes, tubes and channels. Characters in an opium den are always seen sprawling or reclining. In the opening pages of his last, uncompleted novel, *The Mystery of Edwin Drood*, Dickens shows us the 'Princess Puffer', who is based on a well-known East End opium-den proprietor, making up an opium pipe. Her speech, a 'querulous, rattling whisper', has imbibed the sound of the pipes that she makes up for her customers: 'She blows at the pipe as she speaks, and, occasionally bubbling at it, inhales much of its contents'. The opium den is governed by the 'unclean spirit of imitation', in which everything starts to take on the look and shape of everything else, the pipe being the mediator of this ventriloquial interfusion of forms and phonologies.[5]

Where the cigarette becomes a perfect image of the commodity, which consumes itself as it is enjoyed, the pipe is all apparatus, and time apart. The cigarette is direct, disposable, momentary, a kind of oral syringe. The pipe is archaic, auratic, contemplative, ceremonial. Where the cigarette-smoker is drawn out into the thin stream of each successive vanishing puff, the pipe-smoker inhabits a complex, purling backwater of time (pipe-smokers are commonly said to be 'wreathed in smoke'). The design of the hookah pipe allows the smoker to be simultaneously distanced from the source of the smoke and wrapped up inside it. Tenniel's illustration of the hookah-smoking caterpillar perfectly captures this envelopment; the caterpillar squats in languid self-satisfaction atop his mushroom inside the egg-like loop formed by the pipe of the hookah.

The ultimate ambivalence of the pipe is that it is the material relic or correlative of the immaterial smoke, and the pleasure that accompanies it. The pipe, which has so often been fashioned into fantastic anthropomorphic and chimeric semblance, can always aptly bear the caption of Magritte's *The Treachery of Images*: 'Ceci n'est pas une pipe'. The Chinese poet Wang Lu's long poem in praise of his pipe balances material and immaterial, familiarity and inconstancy:

> Out of this emptiness comes the thing of substance:
> My servant boy reverently brings it out.
> Feeling its contours I know instinctively its familiar
> shape…
> I know that there is no constancy in what is possible and
> what is not
> Yet I do not believe that fire and ash are only fragments of
> time…
> Burning and dying out: you alone are my master.[6]

But the smoker's contemplative relation to his pipe is in stark contrast to the death watch unease of the dripping tap and the howling midnight groan of the cooling pipe. The comic catastrophe of an unmoored hosepipe into which water has been forced, bringing about a frenetic, serpentine thrashing and spitting, is an image of the ultimate mastering of the pipe by the flow it is meant to conduct. Bucking, convulsive, with its nozzle spurting like a severed vein, trying to back away from the horror of its own haemorrhage, the hysterically unloosed hosepipe is chaos itself.

14

Plugs

I have in my hand a British three-pin electrical plug. It is smooth, white, hard, odourless. When I hold it, or imagine doing so, my hand takes on the posture of a cardinal performing a benediction. Because this is a British plug, and knowing how to change a plug is the marker of basic practical competence in Britain, I have a clear awareness of what is inside it: the sprung cradle which holds the fuse, the little bar which cinches the top of the cable where it enters the throat of the plug, and the fiddly brass screws sitting atop the three pins, which screw down to grip the three beards of copper wire which I have stripped clear of their outer sheathings of blue, brown and striped green and yellow. Everything has its assigned place in this miniature cosmos, and nothing is interchangeable in its wonderful little engine of stresses, threadings, coercions, couplings and coilings, which requires patience and delicacy to assemble and fold together with maximum efficiency. Knowledge of this interior is denied to the inhabitants of those nations where plugs are sealed and inaccessible.

Plug. It's a word that performs its own nature, the final glottal 'g' chopping off and locking down its sound with a kind of gulp, which happens to be the sound it makes when spelled backwards. It doesn't have a very interesting etymological history, for it cannot be traced much further back than early modern Dutch *plugge*, meaning, simply, a plug, bung or stopper. Still, the importance of the plug to the leaky lowland consciousness, as suggested by the story of the little boy who averts disaster by keeping his finger in the dyke, perhaps makes it appropriate for the word to find its earliest form in Dutch. The word seems to block itself off and plug into itself in the most absolute and obdurate way.

In some places plugs are getting harder to find. Why do airport lavatories, for example, have sinks with no plugs? Nearly always, they also have automatic taps that belch out a grudging little spatter of warm water (or, just as often, don't), when a hand is waved at or under them in a mystic pass. I imagine that it is because airport sinks are the products of the 'defensive design' that characterises most public amenities, a design intended to inhibit rather than to enable the way things offer themselves for our use. The principal concern for the designer of an airport lavatory is that passengers will be getting off planes crumpled and malodorous, and may want to treat the public lavatory like a private washroom, filling the sinks with steaming water, stripping to the waist and turning the paper towels into improvised flannels to give themselves bracing scrub-downs. Surely, the reasoning goes, if the flow of water has to be renewed every few seconds, and no accumulation of water is possible in the sink, this kind of behaviour can be discouraged.

I admit that I have myself, in grimmer, grimier moments, been tempted by the prospect of such a public ablution. But what I mostly need to do in an airport lavatory is ping out my contact lenses, if it is before a long flight, or reinsert them, if I have just disembarked. Where the plughole would be in a domestic sink, there is in the plugless sink a little circular grating, with holes small enough to prevent the loss of rings, but large enough (or just about, I fear) for a contact lens to slip through. So I have to improvise some kind of plug (since I have never been a regular enough traveller to invest in a universal sink plug, which will allegedly cover any hole, though, in any case, the designers of airport lavatories are on to that, for most plugs of this kind require some minimal kind of depression in which to sit, and the plughole of the airport lavatory sink is quite flat). A paper towel will do, though because it quickly gets waterlogged, the glossy front page of a flight magazine is best.

But I see a larger purpose here than merely discouraging stand-up strip-washing or elaborate optical toilette such as mine. The aversion to plugs is part of a more allegorical abhorrence of slowness and lingering. For airports are places of universal, regulated glissando, where the aim is to keep everything smoothly, frictionlessly, and at an even tempo on the move. An airport wants to represent itself as a place with no sharp corners or declivities, no dubious alcoves, no niches in which stuff can accumulate and start to decay and age. A sink brimming with scummy water is a nauseous affront to a place that wants to suggest that everything is just passing smoothly through, without delay or obstruction. I suppose this is also why the lavatories in airports nowadays flush automatically at regular intervals, with or without human occupants, in a parody of the one who nervously wees whether they need to or not (such loos actually sometimes discharge climactically when you are sitting on them).

And yet, despite all this, the paradoxical thing is that an airport is itself nothing but a huge cistern, that sucks people up in great masses, swills them around with nothing much to do for hours, and then suddenly and ecstatically spits them into the sky. The plugless sink is a utopian disavowal of the entire peristaltic store-and-release metabolism of which the airport consists.

But there is another kind of plug that is getting hard to find in airports. As more and more travellers have laptops, the batteries of which cannot last out the long hours of the flight, we have all grown familiar with the sight of laptop owners anxiously scanning the walls of the terminal at ankle level for power sockets. We know that they must exist, for how else does the floor get cleaned, so where have they hidden them, and why? The fact that electrical outlets are becoming more and more scarce is surely for the same reason that there are no plugs in the lavatory sinks. For where there are power sockets, then owners of laptops will inevitably spot them and latch on for a free infusion of juice. But it is not just the freeloading that is offensive to the airport's *amour propre*. Where the sockets are in their usual place, close to the floor, this will induce suited executives to hunker down cross-legged like medieval tailors to work at their machines, sometimes, where there are double sockets, in incongruously intimate couples. The accumulation of such persons, and the clusters of other users of laptops and, increasingly, of other rechargeable devices who may hang around in their vicinity, waiting for them to shove off so that they can in their turn log on, are another kind of unwanted accumulation or resistance to the genial general flow desired by the airport, and a disturbing human analogy to those accumulations of grey, greasy water.

But these efforts to abolish the plug in certain places only serve to highlight the ineffaceable prominence of the plug in our practical and imaginative lives. Plugs plug you in to a particular locality and lifespan. Growing up in Britain, I am used to the three-pin electrical plug I began by eulogising (though I can also just about remember that they used to have round pins). There is something satisfyingly conclusive about the way in which this kind of plug locks into its socket and is clamped tightly in place. I find the two-pin plugs in use throughout most of the rest of the world contemptibly (and alarmingly) loose and approximate in their operation, especially in the US where, unless one inserts the plug with simultaneous decision and precision, and at an angle of precisely 90 degrees to the socket, the act is almost always accompanied by a spiteful little spark and crackle just before the pins go home.

There is a striking dichotomy in the development of the plug and our relationship to it. For centuries, the principal use for plugs has been to stop things up – to seal, to store, or to prevent leakage. Plugs were used to keep food and drink fresh in containers, and to keep the ships that might transmit them watertight. The chemist Robert Boyle's experiments with air and vacuum during the mid-seventeenth century depended upon the capacity to manufacture tightly fitting plugs of different kinds. The word plug was often used to refer to the sucker of a pump, leading to the dialect term 'plugman' for the man who had the vital responsibility for pumping water out of mines. Plugs of this kind and in this era satisfy the instinct for partition, the need and desire to keep unlike things separate and free from contamination. Plugging belonged to a world in which massive moral value was attached to the idea of continence, even if this often went along with a fear of various kinds of stoppage or failure of flow. John Bunyan advised his readers 'Take heed therefore of listning to the charms, wherewith sin inchanteth the soul. In this be like the deaf Adder, stop thine ear, plug it up, to sin: and let it only be open to hear the words of God'.[1]

Plugs also illustrate the hold over the human imagination exercised by the idea of tight and exact fit. When two things come together in this way, the difference between two apparently opposite objects is deliciously annulled, making a single thing out of two. This can be confirmed in the fact that the word 'plug' refers indifferently both to the socket in the wall and the contrivance on the end of the cable that stickler electricians prefer to denominate as the 'plug-top'. There seems a kind of destiny, a sense of utopian consummation, in such perfect experiences of reciprocity, perhaps because things that fit seem to be ideal and absolute rather than off-centre and approximate in the way that nature perversely seems to prefer. That the word 'plug' had a sexual meaning in the nineteenth century should obviously come as no surprise.

The very ubiquity of plugs, bungs and stoppers also meant that they gathered associations that were at once crude and humble. 'Pulling the plug' on something originally referred, not to the breaking of an electrical connection, but to pulling out the stopper that released the liquid in a water closet. To 'plug away' at something does not suggest an operation of very high dignity or finesse. Hamlet imagines in similarly reduced terms the fate of Alexander, ingloriously reduced to plugging a hole after his death:

Why, may not imagination trace the noble dust of Alexander till he find it stopping a bung-hole? ... Alexander died, Alexander was buried, Alexander returneth into dust. The dust is earth, of earth we make loam, and why of that loam whereto he was converted might they not stop a beer-barrel?

> Imperial Caesar, dead and turn'd to clay,
> Might stop a hole to keep the wind away.[2]

When plugs were bungs and stoppers, they were the means of forbidding flow. They maintained a vitalising and sometimes dangerous potential difference between things: on one side of the plug would be wine, on the other side, contaminating air; on our side would be the ship's hold, on nature's, the thirsty salt wave. The plug also established a differential of time. It not only held things apart, it held them up, retarding the natural tendency for things to decay into adulteration.

But this meant that the plughole could also be the cause of sudden inversions or disappearances. The music-hall song 'A Mother's Lament' details one such catastrophe, when an undernourished baby ('nought but a skellington wrapped up in skin') vanishes from the bath when his mother turns round for the soap. In response to her anguished cries the angels reply 'Your baby has gone down the plughole / Your baby has gone down the plug / The poor little thing was so skinny and thin / He should have been bathed in a jug'. Different versions of the final verse emphasise the alternative kinds of other world to which the plughole can give abrupt access, like a wormhole to other dimensions of space and time:

> Don't worry about him, just be happy
> For I know he is suffering no pain.
> Your baby has gone down the plughole
> Let's hope he don't stop up the drain
>
> Your baby is perfectly happy
> He won't need a bath any more
> He's mucking about with the angels above
> Not lost but gone before

But for us, and probably only since the creation of electrical networks at the end of the nineteenth century, the idea of the plug has reversed its meaning. A plug is now not something used to keep things apart, but something that is used to establish connections, to draw together places and times.

Its function is not to inhibit communication but to enable it, not to preserve distinctness, but to establish interchange. In the past, plugs tended to keep the world at bay; now they let it in, or let us into it. We use plugs not to keep things apart, but to become a part of them, to 'plug in' to powers, events, functions, influences. Plugs are scale transformers: they used to keep proximal things distant, now they bring distant things up close. Plugs used to keep things in their place, enforcing a world governed by the prepositions 'in', 'on' or 'at'. Now the plug is the enabler of relationships signified by prepositions like 'through', 'across' and 'between'. In this, one might almost say that the plug is itself a connector between the archaic regime of disconnections and the contemporary regime of connectedness.

The plug that holds in or holds back keeps intact a difference between two distinct things – typically, for example, liquids and the contaminating air from which they are sealed off. In an electrical circuit, there is no such difference, since the point of a plug is to abolish itself; as soon as connection is made, it is as though the plug were no longer there. And yet, although plugs have become universal in the age of electricity, they have never come near to achieving a single, universal form and consequently fading from view. The modularisation of audio playback equipment after the Second World War, which meant that the listening apparatus was distributed between items like turntable, tape deck, tuner, amplifier, speakers and headphones, produced a joyous proliferation of different kinds of plug to connect all these different components together: three-, five- and eight-pin DIN (Deutsches Institut für Normung) plugs, TRS, XLR and RCA (Radio Corporation of America) plugs, along with 'banana plugs'. The multiplication and diversification of TV, video and computer equipment only added to the menagerie, with RF and coaxial, optical fibre and SCART (Syndicat des Constructeurs d'Appareils Radiorécepteurs et Téléviseurs) plugs, all of them, of course, with their mirror image or gendered complementary forms. And, naturally, all these plugs require adaptors to enable them to be plugged into other plugs. Regularly, I find myself standing entranced before the baroque library of copulations ranged before me in the electronics store: RF-SCART, RCA-phono, male-male, male-female, female-female, a fantastic mythical menagerie, unicorn, centaur, mermaid, griffin, liger, tigron, manticore.

Our modern dependence on plugs keeps us earthbound, hooked up like intensive-care patients to life-support systems. For our world is far from being the homogeneous and evenly distributed space that would, in John Donne's words, make 'one little room, an every where'.[3] It is lumpy, clustered, as our own bodies are, focused at particular points of passage and connection, nodes, portals and boreholes which we use to make connections and breakthroughs. Of course an airport is just such a bud, or plug-in point. Without power points and places of connection, we are houseless, amnesic orphans, becoming suddenly aware of the pathetic limits of our internal thesaurus of songs and onboard mental entertainments. We are ourselves leaky vessels, draining sinks, sometimes hearing the gurgles of our own outflow. So, however we might fantasise about a world in which we could be open to ubiquitous energy and data, we know that we need to take every opportunity to engorge our devices with sufficient power to get us through to the next plug-stop.

15

Rubber Bands

 **As I bounced around ideas** about how to begin writing about rubber bands, I caught sight of a rubber-band ball that had been made by one of the administrators in our departmental office. It was quite a modest affair, still only an inch or so across. As I write, the world record is held by a ball made by John Bain which is about 6 feet high and weighs around 3500 lb.[1] The problem with making a rubber-band ball is getting it started. Purists (I realise I am one) will feel that the whole point of the exercise is that it should be entirely self-serving, with the ball being made of nothing but rubber bands all the way down. Of course, you need to make a knot, or create some other kind of primal clot or contusion around which the first rubber band will cling. Thereafter, it will have to cling around itself, but will always have itself to cling around. For those who see nothing wrong with making the first coils around a coin or some other foreign body,

such as compressed tin foil or even another complete rubber ball, there is really nothing to be done. I liken the *ex nihilo* auto-inherence of the rubber-band ball to old-fashioned reel-to-reel tapes, which were held tight on their spools only by the first, infinitesimal friction of the tape on the spool, held down by the many turns of tape that accumulated on top.

Rubber is one of the familiar strangenesses of the modern world. We have become accustomed to the thought that we live in a fundamentally plastic world, one in which we expect materials to be able to be moulded into any shape and consistency. But it may be true in an even more important sense that we live in an elastic world. Elasticity seems magical because it approaches the condition of pure reversibility, in which the energy imparted to an object can be wholly retrieved from it. There can be few cultures and few times in human history in which tone, tension and resilience have not been prized and slackness and sagging deplored and derided. Long before the development of elastic substances, human cultures paid close and admiring attention to the elastic qualities of living beings and of matter, and were glumly observant of the tendency for this elasticity to diminish. 'There is something, I say, irreparable in the Tonical disposition of matter', wrote the seventeenth-century geologist Thomas Burnet.[2] The ideal of absolute elasticity is the dream of a world redeemed from this bitter incorrigibility, in an ideal and absolute 'coefficient of restitution', to borrow the phrase that nineteenth-century physicists P. G. Tait and W. J. Steele gave to the measure of the bounciness of things.[3] It is the promise of return without loss, of a world without withering or decline, in which everything comes back, every expenditure of energy, every deformation or deviation, can be made good.

At least in Europe, the only means of procuring and maintaining elasticity before the development of rubber technologies was by borrowing from natural forms of spring or elastic, such as the springiness of stems and branches, the most important use of which was for longbows and arquebuses. More important were the elastic parts of animals – while they didn't exactly have animal guts for garters, medieval archers made use of the tensile powers of the muscles and fibres of various animals. Nothing was more important in this respect than the skins and bladders of animals, that on the whole had less murderous and more playful uses, for example in fiddle-strings and in the balls, bagpipes and the baubles deployed as professional appurtenances by fools and jesters that we encountered earlier. Robert Boyle was heavily reliant upon the animal bladders (lambs' for preference) supplied by his butcher for his experiments showing what he called 'the spring [that is, the tension or pressure] of the air'.[4]

When artificial means of producing elasticity were procured, they were still dependent upon a natural product, the milky exudations of some 300 different species of tree, of which *Hevea brasiliensis* in the Amazon rainforests gave the most abundant yield. The first explorers and colonists in South America saw natives using the dried residue of this fluid to make waterproof boots, bowls and bottles, which, to the surprise of a French naturalist of the time, Charles-Marie de la Condamine, 'may be squeezed flat, and when no longer under restraint, resume their first form'.[5] Early travellers such as Cortes even saw rubber balls in use for sport in the court of Montezuma II, and noted their superior bounce when compared with the inflated balls in use in Europe.[6]

Several centuries were to elapse before, in the late eighteenth century, the possibilities of rubber began to be explored, at first in France. Joseph Priestley remarked in 1770, in the preface to his book on perspective drawing, that he had seen '*a substance, excellently adapted to the purpose of wiping from paper the marks of a black-lead pencil*'; the substance came to be known as 'lead-eater'.[7] One of the earliest references in English to the elasticity of the substance is in 1785, when one character in Leonard MacNally's comic play *Fashionable Levities* says to another 'you have a convenient conscience, it stretches or contracts like India rubber'.[8] (The designation 'India rubber' almost certainly referred not to India as such, though there was a tree dubbed *Ficus elastica* in Assam which supplied the British with usable rubber, but rather to the products of those other 'Indies' and their 'Indian' peoples, the equatorial regions of Central and South America.) The Montgolfiers' balloon, which made its maiden flight in August 1783, was made of oiled silk or what Benjamin Franklin described as '*taffetas gommé*', silk impregnated with rubber dissolved in linseed oil to help prevent leaks.[9] During the early nineteenth century, the development of rubber products was taken up vigorously in Britain and America, where its forms and uses multiplied.

The first pair of rubber shoes was made available in 1820, by which year the English manufacturer Thomas Hancock had begun manufacturing elasticated gloves, garters, stays and shoes, by sewing into them strips of rubber. Another early use for rubber was for making airtight seals, in the form of stoppers and washers, along with valves of various kinds. Hancock also constructed inflatable life-preservers, along with an air bed, and bags for storing and dispensing gases.[10] The veterinarian Bracy Clark, who was convinced of the cruelty involved in shoeing horses, attempted to match what he believed was the natural elasticity of the horse's foot by a shoe secured with rubber bands – though presumably the stresses to which they were subject made this arrangement impractical.[11] From the late eighteenth century onwards, tubes and pipes made of rubber started to be used in medical and surgical contexts, and rubber hoses became common both in breweries and for fire engines.

There was, however, an intractable problem with rubber, namely that it only retained its elastic properties within quite a narrow range of temperatures. Above 30ºC, rubber started to sag, stick and stink, while, in freezing temperatures, it became rigid and brittle. A story was told of a man who ventured outside wearing a rubber cloak and hat in a freezing New York winter. Finding that the cloak froze solid enough to stand up on its own, he placed his petrified hat upon it and left it outside his front door of his house; taking it for the occupier of the house, passers-by offered the hunched figure respectful salutations.[12] At the other extreme, the Roxbury India-Rubber Company, which experienced a huge boom following its incorporation in 1833, lost two million dollars following a hot summer which melted their products into malodorous treacle.

In the US, Charles Goodyear and, in the UK, Thomas Hancock toiled to overcome this problem. Eventually, it was discovered that impregnating rubber with sulphur enabled it to retain its elasticity across a much broader range of temperatures. Goodyear seems to have discovered the principle first, but it was Hancock who patented and exploited it. He also gave the process its rather colourful name – 'vulcanisation', after the figure of Vulcan, who was associated both with the use of fire and sulphur. He might also have remembered that alchemists' forges were known as the workshops of Vulcan; for the new material seemed to have all the qualities of magical mutability that alchemists sought. Untreated rubber was, so to speak, passively polymorphous; it changed its shape in response to different conditions. But vulcanised rubber was reversibly and controllably polymorphous. It could be mashed up (using a machine invented by Hancock called a 'masticator') and moulded and worked into almost any shape; then, when bent and stretched, it would always return to the shape and condition that had been imparted to it. It was both compliant and resilient. It was not just subject to the changes brought by time, it seemed to have time coiled up in it. It was matter with a memory, though without the inconvenient capacity to learn from experience.

The first patent applied for after the development of the vulcanising process was by Messrs. Perry and Co., in December 1844, 'for the formation of their patent Elastic Bands, which have been so extensively brought into use'.[13] From the 1840s onwards, there was a surge of new applications, including musical instrument components, billiard cushions, nipple shields, bathing caps, baby bouncers and chest expanders.

When it first became common in Europe and America during the early nineteenth century, rubber had all the magic that would later accrue to plastics. Compared to wood or metal, it was easy to shape into almost any form. It absorbed shocks, resisted electric current and repelled liquid. If rubber was infinitely mutable, and could seemingly double or imitate any other form, its malleability, impermeability and elasticity made it ideal for creating tight seals that kept things intact and apart from each other, in particular through providing insulation, in the latex coverings which insulated the submarine telegraph cable laid across the Atlantic in 1857. It was a universal mediator and imitator that itself prevented admixture and adulteration. It seemed to compound the principles of association and separation.

These paradoxes are apparent in a popular article in celebration of rubber which appeared in *Pictorial Half-Hours* in 1850, which remarked on 'how readily it enters into combination with other materials, and imparts to them its own peculiar character of elasticity and imperviousness to moisture. It seems, indeed, as if it were all-penetrating'.[14] As the most essential if also the everyday form of elasticity, the rubber band could come to seem unexpectedly precious, as it does for the narrator of Elizabeth Gaskell's *Cranford*:

> How people can bring themselves to use Indian-rubber rings, which are a sort of deification of string, as lightly as they do, I cannot imagine. To me an Indian-rubber ring is a precious treasure. I have one which is not new; one that I picked up off the floor, nearly six years ago. I have really tried to use it; but my heart failed me, and I could not commit the extravagance.[15]

Grant Allen called rubber 'The Cinderella of Civilisation', because 'it lurks as it were in the back kitchen of invention, and is never in evidence; but it does most of the hard work all the same, and is worthy the diligent quest of the Prince, who detects it at last by the aid of its goloshes'.[16]

So polymorphous was the substance and the forms which rubber could be induced to take that it was not even clear what it should be called. In the early nineteenth century, it was often designated by the name 'caoutchouc', from a Peruvian phrase meaning something like 'the tears of the wood', and the word remained in common use until late in the century. Although the orthography settled down after the eighteenth century, during which variants like 'cahoutchou', 'chaoutchou', 'kahoutchouck', 'caoutchu', 'coatchouc' and 'coutchouc' jostled together, sometimes in the same work, it seems always to have been as much of a mouthful, for the eye as well as the ear, so to speak, as it is now. The eminent mathematician Augustus De Morgan punningly summons the word without actually deigning to mention it in an article of 1871:

> I do not know when the name of *India Rubber* was introduced. Still less do I know when that other name came in, which is enough to choke a cow, and which I never learned to spell. It is not – very properly I think – in the only English dictionary I have at hand, and I will not venture on it.[17]

The first use of the substance as an eraser must have suggested the English word 'rubber', which nearly always appeared in the nineteenth century in the form 'India-rubber'. The insatiable appetite for rubber goods in industrial Britain led to attempts to exploit the equatorial regions of the Far East that were in British control. In an audacious coup, the British naturalist Henry Wickham gathered 70,000 seeds of *Hevea brasiliensis* (which are conveniently propelled from the tree by exploding seedpods) and shipped them back to Kew Gardens, where they produced 2000 seedlings, which were then in turn used to start rubber plantations in Ceylon. Thereafter, they spread throughout Malaya, Indochina and the Dutch East Indies.[18]

Perhaps because of the imperial cast of the English name, the French held on (and still do) to the word 'caoutchouc'. But other terms persisted too, partly because of the confusions that arose between the many forms of gum and resin that were already in use as glues, varnishes and coatings. Rubber was therefore known as 'elastic gum' or 'gum-elastic', terms of which 'chewing gum' and 'gum boots' are the residue, and also 'elastic resin'. The word 'bungee', the origin of which is unknown, was used at the beginning of the twentieth century to refer to rubber erasers, but was transferred to the elastic cords used in the 1930s to launch gliders. The modern sport of bungee jumping, modelled on the vine-jumping ceremonies of New Guinea, was inaugurated on April Fool's Day 1979 by the members of Oxford's Dangerous Sports Club, who leapt off the Clifton Suspension Bridge in Bristol with their ankles tied with elastic ropes, reprising their bouncy plunge off San Francisco's Golden Gate Bridge in October of that year.

The female associations of elastic seem to have been established early. Thomas Haynes Bayly wrote in 1822 of the elastic pull of a woman on a man:

> When near her we are blest – and when we part,
> Elastic fetters twine around the heart:
> Expanding still, the farther we remove,
> Sensitive links extend to those we love:
> They lengthen, strengthen too, – defying fate,
> We prize their pressure, and ne'er feel their weight.[19]

Some time around the middle of the nineteenth century, 'elastic' started to be used as a noun as well as an adjective. If one is to judge from the slightly coy way in which the word is used, it seems to have been identified in particular with the elasticated fabrics that came increasingly to be used in the manufacture of female underclothing. A note on the taking of notes in *Notes and Queries* gave instructions for improvising a simple file produced by a flat board and 'two elastic bands, one longitudinal, the other transverse, not of the India rubber, which are always breaking, but of the material well known to ladies as "elastic."[20] Forty years later, when Grant Allen referred to 'Elastic, in the sense in which ladies use the word, for tying hats and making garters', the feminine associations of the word were evidently still strong.[21]

Elastic has had a huge importance in the transformation of female appearance and possibilities of action. The growth in female participation in competitive sport was very largely due to the radical transformations of underwear brought about by elastics (the 'roll-on corset' which appeared in Britain and the US in 1933, for example), as well as the development of efficient and comfortable fastenings for sanitary pads.[22]

Indeed, although there are masculine forms of elasticated plaything, like the catapult, elastic seems to have a particular prominence in female play. The playground game of French skipping, in which one must hop in and out of tramlines formed by a length of elastic looped round the ankles of two or more playmates, was and doubtless still is overwhelmingly a girls' game. More complex forms of the game might involve the formation of complex cat's-cradle-like reticulations of elastic through supple step overs and rotations on the part of the human posts. The name for the German version of the game, 'Gummitwist', seems to allude to a similar process.

But the most important feature of elastic substance was its association with the body. Just as the bodies of animals had provided the first elastic contrivances, so this arboreal matter complemented and consorted with human bodily forms and functions. Rubber syringes, catheters and clyster bags were in use from the 1770s, and a wide variety of other kinds of rubber pipe and tube quickly became part of medical apparatus in the early nineteenth century. A rubber breast pump was being advertised in 1780, promising that '[T]he large size Bottles are lately fond to draw the Breast much easier than the Mouth, as the Draught is so gentle that it is scarcely felt'.[23] The medical uses of rubber bandages in providing compression and traction, and of elastic stockings to treat conditions such as varicose veins, anticipated the discovery of the protein 'elastin', which is found in skin, bladder and lungs and is particularly concentrated in the veins and heart, where it assists the movements of expansion and contraction required for the circulation of the blood.[24]

The fact that elasticated materials could be made to cling so closely to the body added to the growing feeling that rubber was a kind of body double. Flesh and rubber entered into each other's compositions, giving rise to more and more minglings and affiliations. As late as 1920, rubber bands were being recommended for the removal of tartar from teeth.[25] The fleshy quality of rubber made it the material of choice in the making of automata: the American showman P. T. Barnum exhibited 'Joice Heth', a garrulous old black woman, allegedly 161 years of age, who was in fact an automaton, made of whalebone, india rubber and springs, operated by a ventriloquist.[26] In 1830, a Dr Auzou exhibited in Paris an anatomical model which simulated the process of labour for the benefit of the student: 'By means of caoutchouc and confined air', it was reported, 'he is able to show the expansions and contractions in labour, so as to enable the student to proceed in his practice with confidence and safety'.[27]

Rubber and elastic products helped fill out the indeterminate space between animate entities and inert objects, and the exchanges between the categories were nowhere more developed than in the invention of erotic relations. A naturalist wrote intriguingly in 1774 that 'there is an elastic gum, called Borrachio in Portugese, and Kaoutchuck in the language of the natives near Cayenne in South America of which it is said the Chinese make elastic rings for lascivious purposes'.[28] Maximilian Lamberg goes into a little more detail about these 'Chinese rings', associating them with 'the fruit of a sensitive tree which swells and rebounds from the hand that touches it', along with balls inserted in themselves by the female occupants of seraglios for similar forms of self-satisfaction.[29] The capacity of rubber and elastic to cling to and constrict the flesh both simulated and stimulated the engorgement characteristic of various forms of arousal. Elastic objects embodied the elastic paradox of sexual desire itself, namely that a certain measure of constraint seems essential to it.

The advantages of rubber for the manufacture of contraceptive sheaths became apparent early, and rubber quickly displaced the animal tissues that had previously been in use – the best-adapted but also the most expensive being the bladders of a certain fish caught in the Rhine. In his *Medical Common Sense* of 1863, Edward Bliss Foote described the operations of what he called the 'womb-veil', consisting of 'an India-rubber contrivance which the female easily adjusts in the vagina before copulation, and which spreads a thin tissue of the rubber before the mouth of the womb so as to prevent the seminal aura from entering'.[30] Foote thought he had invented this device, though the idea had occurred to others, such as the German gynaecologist Friedrich Adoph Wilde, who described a rubber diaphragm in 1838.[31] The opposition to contraception in the US anyway meant that Foote never patented the device, meaning that the female diaphragm was developed elsewhere, principally in the Netherlands, so that it became known in consequence as the Dutch Cap. In this form, the device had been made much safer and more effective through the addition of a sprung rubber rim.

The eroticism of rubber helps to give it magical qualities, and, as it became more familiar, it began to show another of the characteristic signs of a magic substance, namely that its physical qualities started to seep into the very ways in which it was imagined and described. Conceptions of elastic started to become as stretchy as the substance itself. Thomas Hancock records that the range of uses for this adaptable substance struck one old gentleman who saw a specimen of it as itself infinitely elastic: 'when exhibiting a piece of my solid rubber to an old gentleman, he examined it, and on returning it made this remark (which bids fair to be realised): "*The child is yet unborn who will see the end of that*".[32] Grant Allen introduced his essay in praise of india rubber with the warning '[t]he subject of this article is going to be india-rubber. The reader must therefore not be astonished if my treatment of it at first appears a trifle elastic. Who drives fat oxen must himself be fat, and who writes of rubber must himself be expansive'. True to his warning, his essay wanders in a leisurely way into discussions of flint, glass and other substances, concluding that no substance can really be regarded as wholly indispensable for the development of civilisation, but then pinging his discourse back on itself to proclaim 'the indispensability of rubber'; Allen then defiantly suggests that the only way for somebody to be cured of the intellectual rigidity of seeing this as inconsistent would be 'by getting an india-rubber brain extension'. Rubber enters into the composition of the very words which evoke its condition – 'the written word is just like india-rubber', wrote Allen, 'it goes everywhere, and is applied to all sorts of unexpected purposes'.[33] Perhaps the rubber band is the exemplar of this universal adaptability. Before the arrival of Perry's rubber bands in the 1840s, a 'rubber band', or an 'elastic band', was either sewn into a hat, shoe or glove, or was itself an article with a specific use, like the corset advertised by the Edinburgh corset-maker Mrs Draffen, who advertised in 1834 'her Elastic INDIA-RUBBER BAND, which, for the elegance it gives to the shape, and the comfort it imparts to the wearer, will be found invaluable'.[34] Thereafter, the rubber band became a kind of all-purpose object, which was not definitively for any one thing in particular, but rather embodied a kind of universal adaptability. It is not surprising that so many uses have been found for rubber bands, from stringing biscuit-tin banjos to powering model aircraft. Unlike some objects, like spoons and pens, which I buy regularly, but which always seem to be in short supply, I cannot ever remember buying elastic bands, though they always seem to be ready at hand. This abundant supply may ultimately be guaranteed by the postmen's habit of strewing the streets with the elastic bands that have secured their bundles of mail.

When Charles Goodyear, whose life and fortunes were entirely consumed in the passion for rubber, published his personal account of his travails and visions for the '[t]his substance … as wonderful and mysterious as any in nature',[35] he insisted that his book be, as one reviewer put it, 'self-illustrating', inasmuch as 'treating of India-rubber, it is made of India-rubber'. The pages of the book, 'thinner than paper, can be stretched only by a strong pull, and resume their shape perfectly when they are let go' (librarian readers may be relieved to know that I refrained from this experiment with the copy I consulted in the British Library).[36]

The multiplication of elastic substances has made for a growing elasticity in the very idea of substance. No longer is the world made up of and divided into elements with invariant, indwelling properties. Rather, our world is one in which every substance varies under different conditions. The blind polymath John Gough discovered early in the nineteenth century that, where most solids expand when they are heated, elastic materials in fact contract when they are heated; conversely, and equivalently, when they are stretched, they give off heat, a fact that can be confirmed in the same way as Gough confirmed it, by holding an elastic band to your lips, then stretching it, which will cause the band to feel warmer.[37] The explanation for this involves the association of heat with molecular disorder. The molecules of rubber are tangled round each other in a high state of disorder. Extending the band lines the molecules up in an orderly way, which means that it gives off heat. Subjecting an elastic band to heat, by contrast, increases the disorder of the molecules, which means that it will tend to move from a stretched, orderly state, to a contracted, disordered state.

Elasticity is the movement of substances between conditions, it is substance become circumstantial. It all now, like the dangling bungee jumper, depends.

And yet, nowadays, there is usually something melancholy and grotesque about rubber, which has come to seem more like an ugly residue from a brave new world that has grown newly old. Like the rubber band itself, rubber has started to recoil on itself. There had always been a violent side to the contractive powers of rubber, which can sting as well as sing. One of the earliest responses to elastic clothing is an anonymous little squib entitled 'A Thought on an Elastic Hat Band', which compared the tight embrace of the elasticated hat to that of a noose:

> Whenever a band like this I see,
> I straight do make a simile:
> An halter, that elastic string,
> It to my mind does always bring.
> And critics sure will this permit,
> One every head, one every neck will fit![38]

A similar thought occurred to the contributor to *Notes and Queries* who commented in 1860 on the recent appearance of a new childish weapon, or a new form of an old one, in that it made use of the propulsive force of elastic, the catapult. The article concluded that 'it would appear that in the judgment of the "Dark Ages," the best remedy for the unlawful use of the catapult was a *rope's end*. Has the hint no significance now?'[39] According to the Mexican Jesuit Francisco Clavigero, rubber was involved in human sacrifice among the Totonaca people of Mexico, the high priest being anointed with 'elastic gum mixed with children's blood'.[40] Violence had lain latent in latex for a long time.

The rubber objects that once seemed to epitomise the modern can now often seem sad, sinister, comical or perverse. The very process of vulcanisation, which seemed to render rubber so durable, now makes disposing of waste rubber products, especially of the seventy per cent of rubber products that form tyres and other automobile components, very difficult.[41]

A rubber-band ball itself effects a reversal, because it takes one kind of elasticity and turns it into another. Before the development of elastic materials, elasticity tended to mean suppleness, buoyancy, bounce or spring, that which recoiled when compressed, rather than that which sprang back after being stretched. A rubber ball bounces when it meets another object or surface. A rubber band springs back to its original shape after it has been stretched. In the one case the bounce is expansive and often unpredictable; in the other it is conservative and reliable. The rubber band merely, if sometimes violently, comes back to itself; in its way of coming back to itself, a rubber ball goes somewhere else. But the two kinds of elasticity come together in loop quantum cosmology, also known as the Big Bounce theory of the universe, which suggests that, rather than expanding indefinitely, the gravity of the universe will eventually, at the fullest extent of its stretch, start to pull back in on itself. But then, at the other extreme, rather than concertinaing back to a singularity, quantum effects will cause the universe to bounce back and start expanding again. This is not the only way in which rubber bands exert their pull on thinking on the grandest scale. But rubber bands have also been implicated in the imagination of the infinitesimally small. String theory proposes that the ultimate constituents of matter are loops, or strings which twist, stretch and collide, the different frequencies at which they oscillate producing what we detect as electrons, quarks, neutrinos and other subatomic particles. The joint originator of string theory, Leonard Süsskind, first envisaged them not as strings, but rather as tiny, singing rubber bands.[42]

16

Sticky Tape

 **Childhood is,** superbly and self-evidently, an epoch of stickiness. Children are magnificently apt to get into a sticky condition, their fists, faces and clothes seemingly having the power to retain traces of everything with which they come into contact. The stickiness that provokes disgust in adults provokes fascination and delight in children. The winners in a recent TV game show in which the contestants had to produce and successfully market a new product were a group of women who devised a children's suit made of velcro. Wearing the suits, children were able literally to bond and disband with each other, as though joining and tearing off their skins.

But the stickiness of childhood has a larger, more philosophical significance. The day when one starts to find the sticky icky is the day that one starts to unpeel from childhood. Stickiness is the opposite of autonomy, for it advertises your surface, indeed reduces you to it, so that you seem to be possessed of no private depth or interiority. A sticky creature is a contingent, adjacent, epidermal creature, which carelessly and helplessly picks up and displays the marks of anything that just happens to happen to it. This is why stickiness is humiliating in an adult – why it is an acknowledged social duty to rescue a friend from the shame of walking round all day with a smear of chocolate or toothpaste around their mouth. To bear such an unwitting smirch, especially on one's face, is to have surrendered one's sovereign power and responsibility of self-super-vision; to seem not to have oneself in view is to be reduced to the condition of an object in the field of view of others. One of the classic tests for self-consciousness in animals is to make a mark on the animal's face and place it in front of a mirror – if it reaches for the mark or tries to remove it from its own person, it may be said to have consciousness of itself. This is why tarring and feathering is the ultimate painless torture; to be feathered is to be made to flourish the signs of your stickiness. As a treacled pseudo-turkey you are no longer anything essential, but only an accident-prone outside. Stickiness is parasitic, and indeed many parasites use mechanisms of adhesion to latch and hang on to their hosts. Of course, when we leave behind the stickiness of childhood, we also leave behind the miraculous capacity for unconscious and effortless learning that is its cognitive complement; we may no longer walk around casually emblazoned with the residue of toffees and candyfloss, but equally we cannot any more spontaneously *pick up* knowledge and skills, like teasel-burrs, in the way in which children cannot but help.

So at home are children in stickiness that it becomes a sovereign principle for them. One of the consequences of the child's high tolerance of stickiness is the unrealistically high degree of trust they retain in the powers of glue and other agents for sticking things together. Having once discovered the powers of glue, children are loath to give up the theory that anything can be stuck in place, or put back together again, with it, or with cognate substances. Stickiness and glueiness are, for children, not signs of corruption or mess, as they may be for adults, but of the reparability, maybe even the ultimate redeemability, of matter; perhaps the ultimate model for this is the glueiness of young flesh, which promptly and invisible mends every gash.

Seen from the phobic adult side of things, the principal quality of stickiness starts to be its invasiveness. As the principle of displacement, stickiness itself does not lurk in one spot, but spreads. A jar of honey that is not perfectly clean on the outside will sweat and diffuse its stickiness, until there is a perfectly uniform ring of honey around its base, locking it to the shelf. Unless I clean and dry it perfectly, the slightly gelatinous liquid that has rilled down the outside of my bottle of contact lens conditioner will do the same in the bathroom cabinet. The mode of the sticky is ooze, reluctant but unrelenting. In characterising the quality that he famously called the *visqueux*, which is usually translated, not quite accurately, as the 'slimy', Jean-Paul Sartre represented it as a kind of interrupted or corrupted flow; where water flows evenly and predictably, slimy stuff is 'an aberrant fluid ... the dawning triumph of the solid over the liquid ... the agony of water'.[1] Stickiness is a vitiated stillness, a solidity infected by slow, syrupy drift, in an insidious conspiracy of the liquid with the solid. It sticks to itself, and sticks other things to it, but its stickiness is a seduction and a solicitation rather than a threat; one can always and easily break the glutinous bond which it intimates, but only at the cost of having oneself become sticky. Or, as we tellingly tend to say, 'all sticky', since stickiness does nothing by halves, and to be a little sticky is always to be overtaken and obsessed by it.

Childhood is sticky, in that it is turned adhesively towards the world; adulthood is sleek, in that it faces inwards, in the direction of inherence rather than adherence. Providentially, these two orders or epochs of things are ideally conjoined in sticky tape. On one side, the tape is hard, glossy and tractable, like the ideal objects of the adult world; on the other, it is matt, sticky and entangling. The purposive is here twinned with the accidental. The smooth side vouchsafes a world of distinct bodies, where things stay put, keeping themselves to themselves; the stickiness speaks of a world that promiscuously commingles. Oddly enough, therefore, the shiny side of things is the one where things stick together or sustain themselves, where the sticky side is the side of impermanence, in which things are never quite or wholly themselves. Sticky tape is magical because it promises that the two sides of the world, the two orders of things, the smooth and the sticky, the distinct and the indistinct, can themselves miraculously be articulated, which is to say, both kept distinct and yet also joined together. Like so many other apparently unremarkable objects, the roll of sticky tape is a philosophical machine.

Which means that, like all machines, especially philosophical ones, it does not always function perfectly, partly because it starts to mate with or mutate into itself. Unless one makes a little hem at the end after using it, to furnish a handle for the next visit, the cellulose may often mysteriously bind together, seemingly melting into itself, leaving no leading edge apparent, no matter how infuriatedly we may rotate the roll. Vision is of little use in this endeavour. All of us know the futile routine you have to adopt, without knowing how or when we acquired it. With one hand, you play the roll through the other hand, while applying a thumbnail or index fingernail to the surface rolling underneath it. The nail has to act as a kind of gramophone stylus, listening as much as feeling for the delicious, decisive little notch that will let you back in to the locked problem of the tape. There are all kinds of false alarms, since a roll of sticky tape that has fused with itself in this condition has also usually developed ridges and ripples, like the glass in an ancient window, and this can generate humiliating jubilations. But just finding the tiny ledge is not enough. For if you rush at it, hooking up a little corner and pulling too excitedly, you run the risk of tearing away only a thin strip, that is much less than the width of the whole roll, which either diminishes to nothing in the space of a full rotation, leaving only a pitiful little sticky thread between finger and thumb, or carries on unpeeling for several rotations of the roll. There is now nothing to be done but to put the roll down flat on the top of a table and scrape your nail downwards on to the ridge that is now running horizontally along the middle of the roll, in the hope of being able to break into it that way. Even if one finally succeeds, the victory will be tainted with the misery and mess of the process.

This technique is not the only sticky tape tactic we must learn. To apply a strip of sticky tape to a torn map, for example, requires a complex cooperative dance between the different parts of the hand and finger. First of all, a strip of tape of approximately the right length must be snipped, ripped or bitten off. Then, you must line the strip up with the tear. But the tear will also need to be secured by applying pressure and just a little bit of lateral stretch, to make sure that the edges to be mended abut each other, with edge placed precisely against edge. It is best for this to be done with the outsides of the little fingers of the two hands, which must secure the map until the very moment before the tape makes contact. The most successful results come, not from placing the middle of the tape in the middle of the tear, and, releasing the ends, smoothing it outwards from the middle, but advancing the tape as close as possible to the tear, and then simply dropping it. This tiny hesitation before the tape is dropped into place is full of trepidation, for one can never in fact be absolutely sure that the perfect alignment will be maintained, that the stickiness of the sticky tape will not itself bring about some kind of distorting drag.

The word 'Sellotape' was adapted from 'cellophane' by Colin Kininmonth and George Gray, who bought a French sticky-tape patent in 1937 and developed it for the British market. At a stroke it thereby gained a vital connection to the powerful – and ancient – material imagination of sealing. For sticky tape does not merely join or seam; much more important is its function of wrapping, insulating and closing off. Sealing does more than repair; it preserves and even, in a sense, renews things. Sealing belongs to an extensive ecology of imaginary, vitreous second skins, which, by doubling the objects they enclose, seem to have the power to confer on them a kind of clarity and self-sufficiency that was previously lacking to the original object. To shrink-wrap a foodstuff seems somehow both to dignify and perfect it. The seal impressed into the sealing wax affirms the authenticity and entirety of the document, by imparting to it an authority that comes from somewhere else – the seal, as it were, is a consummating knot, that brings the document together with itself. The transparent seal seems to double the object with itself, wrapping it in a second skin that is nothing but a lustre, affirming that it is what it is, both transparent and impermeable, original and uncorrupted.

But there is a subtle misery ticking away in this transfiguring second skin of cellophane, or Sellotape. For sticky tape, we know, decays, in ways that sadly and alarmingly resemble the deterioration of human skin. It grows dry and brittle, and loses its stretch and adhesiveness, curing in time to a rancid toenail-yellow. Eventually, it will snap or crumble. The problem of how to remove adhesive tapes from objects in art and library collections that had been optimistically mended and preserved by it, but have now begun to deteriorate, is a serious one.[2] As it crisps, curls and flakes, losing both its spring and its grip, it seems to remind us of the organic basis of the sticky. The 'glutinous' recalls the glue boiled up from hooves and hides of animals, yielding a gelatin that could be mixed with water again to make glue; the 'viscous' the stickiness of sap and resin, originally from the Latin *viscus*, the mistletoe, the berries of which were used to make birdlime. Stickiness is itself sticky with reminiscence of amphibious bodily fluids like sperm, sputum, spittle and snot.

As though in confirmation of these resemblances between sticky tape and bodily fluids, the very first adhesive tapes were designed for medical uses, for example in the tapes and bandages smeared with starch and gum used by physicians in Ancient Egypt. Surgical bandages, made of fabrics smeared with fat and honey, were in use around 1500 BC, and the 'diachylon' bandage, or 'lead-plaster', using an adhesive made of olive oil mixed with lead oxide, devised in Ancient Greece, continued to be used well into the twentieth century. The development of adhesive tape was carried forward almost entirely in the medical sphere, through improvements in plasters and adhesive dressings. In 1791, a C. Grossant devised a technique which used the first rubber-based adhesive in surgical tape.[3] When the first patent for a pressure sensitive tape was taken out by W. H.

Shecut and Horace H. Day in 1845, it was for an improved surgical plaster.[4]

It was not until the following century that industrial and domestic uses for adhesive tape began to be met and invented. In 1925, Richard G. Drew, of the Minnesota Mining and Manufacturing Company (3M), adapted the principle of surgical tape to create masking tape that allowed two-tone cars to be sprayed with sharp dividing lines between the two colours. The most important feature of the new product was its reversibility: the tape would not only keep the two colours separate from each other, without the leaking or bleeding that fabric tapes allowed, it could also be removed once the paint was dry, without damaging the surface or leaving a residue. It has been suggested that the tape came to be known as 'Scotch Tape' because in the early days the manufacturers tried to save money by stingily only coating the outer edges of the tape with adhesive. In 1930, Drew found a way to coat transparent cellophane with adhesive and the result was marketed as Scotch® Cellophane Tape. The transparency of the tape was adventitious; Drew hit on it originally as a way of making a completely waterproof tape for protecting insulating material from moisture. The Goodyear Zeppelin Corporation wrapped large amounts of Scotch tape round the interior struts of their airships to protect them from corrosion. The appearance of the tape at the beginning of the depression helped turn what would otherwise have been rather a specialist, luxury product into an all-purpose way for thrifty Americans to make-do-and-mend.[5]

The experience of sticky tape, the bodily intuitions and intrigues it teaches us, cannot be understood in terms of vision and tactility alone. For sticky tape also has its own distinctive repertoire of sonorities. There is the subtle judder or clicking of the fingernail against the ridge formed by the end of the tape, and the range of different kinds of snap as the tape is separated from itself in different ways – snipped by scissors, torn by front teeth, tugged messily apart. Most distinctive of all, there is the ecstatic ripping sound as the tape is pulled away from the roll, a sound that can itself be modulated in frequency and timbre by variation in the force applied, rising from the soft sizzle of a slow, even haul to the almost soprano shriek of the most vigorous yank. It has been known since the 1930s that pulling away adhesive tape in the dark can produce a faint flash of luminescence.[6] More recently, Seth Putterman of the University of California at Los Angeles has shown that peeling off sticky tape at 3 centimetres a second can generate a blast of X-rays powerful enough to photograph the bones of your hand.[7]

There is an ambivalent delight in the pulling of sticky tape away from itself that foreshadows and is recalled by the pleasure of pulling it away from the surfaces on to which it has been stuck, especially the skin. Ripping quickly and intemperately provides an invigorating severity, the tearing terror of a sabre slash without the pain or injury. But pulling sticky tape away from the skin slowly is the connoisseur's way. First of all, a whole hank of skin is lifted, and then, as it seems, pore by pore, and hair by hair, it gradually relinquishes its hold, falling back to itself. Either way, the peeling away of the sticky tape allows the fantasy of a sanitising, renewing dermabrasion, a restoring of the skin to its idealised newness and tenderness. In depilatory waxing, and the use of sticky tape to remove fibres from clothing, this promise is made actual. It can be no surprise that sticky tape, and its family of allied tapes, duct tape, gaffer tape, masking tape, play such a vigorous and versatile role in fetishistic sexual fantasy.

Stickiness has gathered a new value in our culture of surf and glide. Web forums and blogs can post headers to each page called 'stickies', that maintain their position as the other entries scroll away downwards. Web designers aim to make their pages and sites 'sticky', in a similar sense, meaning that users will tend to keep coming back to them; the stickiness of a commodity or object will be the measure of how indispensable it may come to seem to its owner. We can never leave stickiness entirely behind. It clings to us as the bubblegum to the foot-sole, the flypaper to the fly. Is it ourselves that we cannot quite shake off and find hard to leave in stickiness?

17

Sweets

So great a sweetness flows
I shake from head to foot.[1]

Yeats

The most magical objects of all are objects that
do something to us, and seem to have their own
lives, even if they are also lives that we can control. Perhaps all such
objects are things that we dream of ultimately making part of us, or
dream actually already are. And perhaps the most magical of these
objects are those which we can actually incorporate and make part
of ourselves, in the process effecting changes in them and in us.
Edible objects are of this kind, though we would be wrong to think
that we only ingest actual objects. There is an imaginary form of
swallowing up and incorporation for every object that is important
to us, for every object that we think of as amenable or pleasurable.
We appear to be the kind of beings for whom a pleasurable or

important object must always be in some sense also edible.

Sweets engender a whole lifestyle, a whole ethnology of their own. Everybody participates in the collective mythology attaching to sweets from their own childhood, and everybody has their own personal ethics and principles for eating them. Adverts often focus on these individuating methods for consuming particular sweets, and incommunicable pleasures in eating them, suggesting that a sweet is not so much an object, as a whole repertoire of eating techniques (Cadbury's Creme Eggs are marketed with the slogan 'how do you eat yours?').

Doing magic is a way of insisting that the world is not neutral, but pulsing with human meaning and value. And there is no form of value, no taste, more important than the value of the sweet. What is sweetness? Sweetness is not just one taste among others, not just a good taste. It is the taste of goodness as such, the measure of edibility. Sweetness is the good of eating. This is why sweetness is always more than taste. Being the essence of taste makes sweetness also gratuitous, luxurious. At the same time, or at other times, it also makes it dangerous, disreputable, disallowed.

Sweets and sweetness are the essence of eating. But this is why we do not want to swallow sweetness, because we know that swallowing is its end. If sweetness has evolved in plants and fruits in order to encourage consumption, just as sexual attractiveness is there to honey copulation, then in humans sweetness is perverse, turned aside from its seemingly proper end or purpose. We want to keep sweetness apart from the vulgarity of hunger and the utilitarian purposes of nutrition. There is surely something intemperate about sweet-eating, which can approach alcohol in addictiveness. This makes it a little odd that sweet-making has been associated in both Britain and the

US with Quakers – the three principal manufacturers of chocolate in Britain, Fry, Cadbury and Rowntree, were all Quaker concerns, and Good and Plenty, the first branded candy in the US, was produced in 1893 by the Quaker City Confectionery Company. This is partly because chocolate, which was originally consumed as a drink, could be offered as a temperance alternative to strong liquor.

'Don't play with your food', adults say to children. But sweets are made to be playthings, protests against the sensible good citizenship of eating routines. Perhaps this is also why we treat sweets as playthings. Sweets are things that we do things to. We want to handle them before we commit them to our tongues, where we play with them anew. Are there any more elaborately erotic coverings than the wrappers of sweets, waxy, crackling, filmy-wrinkled? Sweets systematically break the gustatory rule that once something is in your mouth it must stay there until it is swallowed, since, once in your mouth, food has already started to become a kind of excrement. But sweets are meant to come and go, to go in and out. Sweets are the only kind of food that we are allowed to see the results of eating. They give us access to an otherwise most secret and invisible process, the process of rendering something that is part of the outside world part of us. The multilayered lolly or lozenge encourages us to keep taking it out to see what colour it has changed to, in a striptease for the taste buds. Chewing gum and bubblegum are never swallowed at all, and are therefore perhaps the most essential kind of sweet. Once we have had the sweetness from it, the substance of the gum is a mere nothing, or nothing but play.

Sweets are beyond words. All sweets are gobstoppers. When we eat sweets, we say 'mmm', the sound of speech's superseding, the replacing of speaking by sweetness. Or perhaps it is truer to say that sweets are the rivals of speech. They encourage the production of an alternative language, one made up of slurps and slobbers, suckings, dribbles, pops and crunches; all of this an oozing, elemental anti-language that is most of the time kept inaudible, or disciplined into speech. Sweets let us hear all the things you are never allowed to hear in the radio voice. Sweet talk is also, of course, baby talk, an infant and infantilising language, which is on the border between eating and speaking, and lets us hear eating, and eat meaning. The words 'gum' and 'gobstopper' clog and glue the mouth like the things they name. The words 'jelly' and 'lolly' and 'lollipop' elicit lolling and licking from the tongue that lets them out. Even the grown-up names of sweet makers and sweet owners become suffused with magical, nestling comfort. You could never, I think, take a philosopher called Cadbury seriously (I know, I know, saying this in public means I am bound straight away to hear of, or worse, from one), but if a Cadbury should ever run for prime minister in Britain, they would surely be unopposable. Even though sweets may be beyond words, the language of sweets is a vital part of their power. The names of sweets often hint at sublimity or transcendence; 1960s sweets in particular suggest fantasies of cosmic reach, *Milky Way*, *Mars*, *Galaxy*, albeit with the slightly antique cast that the idea of outer space now has. To hear such words on the lips of a grown-up, or to hear them in one's own mouth, is to be in two places, or two times, at once; to surrender to the indignity and bliss of infancy. All magical objects are objects out of time. Sweets hold time up, and therefore are intensely anachronistic. They always belong to our past. They help us last.

We seek to detain sweetness. Sweetness is identified with the excess of taste over aliment, and therefore with the pleasure of pro-longing itself. That is why so many sweets are designed to be held in the mouth – or, in a perverse reversal of the perverse desire to hold back consumption in the sweet, to melt, yearningly and disappointingly on the tongue, in a brief sweetness which becomes the very sweetness of the brief. Sweets are parables of finitude. In learning how to make sweetness last, children learn on their tongues the lesson of deferment, of holding on, and holding off, upon which all cultural life, and perhaps all life as such, is based.

Sweetness is so important to us that it generates rituals and protocols. Sweets are surrounded by complex rules and prescriptions, the infallible signs of the presence of magic. They are also, despite their role in rituals of exchange, intensely private, the stuff of dark and unmasterable addictions and obsessions; and also, for children at least, intensely social. Sweets function as the universal medium of exchange, a kind of *manna* or *mana*, an all-purpose magical stuff for building and cementing alliances, sealing treaties and treasons, feuds and affiliations.

Sweet-making and sweet-eating are closely and mysteriously associated with the arts of magical picturing and effigy. We eat things we like the look of; teddies, bunnies and gingerbread men. Themed birthday cakes give us the opportunity of eating ourselves: the Arsenal supporter, or the *Thomas the Tank Engine* fan, eats their loved object, and encounters anew its sweetness. This is as it should be, for sweet things really do not taste of themselves; they taste of our own pleasure in them. We also eat in the form of sweets things that we fear and loathe, but seem to wish to neutralise by consuming: spiders, snakes, insects, dinosaurs – even, in a bizarre, unaccountable but stubbornly persistent British tradition, mechanical tools. It is as though we were celebrating our capacity to render the whole world fit for our consumption.

The shape and texture of a sweet, its characteristics as an object, are vital supplements to its taste. Why does it matter so much that a Kola Cube is crunchy, that a Walnut Whip has the striations it does, that a Milky Bar is so snappy-thin, that a Toblerone is, as the advertisement has it, 'triangular chocolate'? Why does the shape of a sweet matter so much? It is because sweets are there to have their shapes transformed. As Willy Wonka and Alice knew, their meaning is pure metamorphosis. Through sweets, more than any other eatable, we enact the experiencing of merging and dissolution. Sweets are magical objects, because their shape is there to be transformed, to transform themselves under our touch. They are subtle, paradoxical, alchemical, polymorphous substances. Sweets are designed to suggest matter in extreme or ultimate conditions: iron-hard in the case of the aniseed ball, sludgy and viscous in the form of fudge, fizzy and explosive like sherbet, clinging and elastic like toffee, spun and insubstantial like candyfloss. They are as heavy as mud and as light as air, savagely hot and tooth-jarringly chill. We like sweets that are latticed with holes or bubbles, because they seem to let us taste vacancy. Their colours are like nothing ever seen in nature and represent a victory over it. Sweets provide a kind of gustatory pyrotechnics, and sweets are closely allied to fireworks. No wonder cartoons are used to sell sweets, because sweets are the cartoons of eating experience. But sweets don't only represent matter in extremity; they also enact the promiscuous coupling of different substances. The very stickiness of sweets is a triumph over distinctions and codes of polite behaviour designed to keep things apart and in their proper places. They are what may be called 'mingled bodies': jelly beans, dolly mixtures, baked alaska, liqueur chocolates.[2] It is not for nothing that the makers of sweets bear the noble name of 'confectioners', literally, those who make things come together.

Sweets mean and enact flowing, dissolving, merging, metamorphosis. Why so many explosions, so many bombs bursting in the air in the names of sweets (Starbursts, Fizzers, Sherbert Fountains, the Snap and Crackle, the Wham bar), why so many teasing deceits and promises of amazement and teeming transmogrifications in their manufacture (Curly-Wurlies, Fried Eggs and Live Wires), if we are not really always saying to sweets and they to us: 'Surprise!' Sweets will let nothing persist as what it merely, drearily, is.

Perhaps this is part of the reason why eating sweets is not meant entirely to be a pleasure. In the eating of a sweet, the entire being is concentrated around the drawing out of the taste. Look at somebody who has just got the first sour spurt out of a sherbet lemon, or the spreading drowsiness of a lump of milk chocolate. The eyelids are flickering, the eyes misting like a junkie's after a hit. There is nothing there but ardour, ordeal, and the sweet toil of bliss. Sweets challenge and provoke us: 'Eat me', they say. And then they eat us back. It seems right that sweet-eating should be such a risk, that sugar should damage our teeth. Pills are so easily mistaken for sweets, because they are designed to look like them, to remind us of the narcotic potency of sweets.

If sweets have about them a generalised kind of perversity, they are also like sexual perversions in being intensely specific. I have said nothing, because I know next to nothing, of girls' sweets – Love Hearts and the like. Have I dreamt this, or did they not use to wear necklaces and bracelets *made out of sugar*, that would linger diminishingly through the day? And then there are aunties' and grannies' sweets: Parma Violets and other enigmatic perfumed stuff, living amid hankies in bags. Mystery, mystery. This is another reason why the language of sweets makes all the difference. When Mars decided to rationalise the nomenclature of its international product range, Opal Fruits became Starbursts, and in the process became an entirely different product and experience. There is a fundamental distinction between the Anglo-European and American metaphysics of confectionery, a distinction marked by the difference between the two words 'candy' and 'sweets'. Candy suggests a single, amorphous, all-purpose substance, or sweet-essence, which is moulded into different forms. In British English, there is no such essence, no quiddity; sweets are just that, sweets, in the plural, a plenitude of uncommutable singularities. But the thing that all English-speaking sweets have in common is that no one sweet resembles any other. In sweets, we live out a world of pouring plurality. *Allsorts*.

18

Wires

 **The sociable motto** offered by E. M. Forster in his novel *Howards End* seems to apply everywhere today, but with a different meaning: 'only connect'.[1] Nowadays, getting a connection tends to mean hooking up to a network, rather than necessarily establishing any physical link. Ours is a world increasingly of wireless rather than wired connections. In fact, the dream of dispensing with wires is an old and recurrent one. The wireless world that opened up at the beginning of the twentieth century was going to be a world of communications effected by waves, radiation, vibration, emanation; we would live as the angels had once been thought to live, in a world of instantaneously transmitted thoughts and impulses. The wireless world promised to cut our connection to the sluggish and impeded and annoyingly chopped-up world of time and place and bodies and distances and matter.

Wires and waves are very different things. A world of communication by waves and vibrations and emanations is a world of permeated lives, in which individual identities are dissolved, ecstatically or uneasily as it may be, in universally shared experiences. A world of communication along wires offers the delights of communication across vast distances, but with the preservation of intimacy and secrecy. The person on the end of the telephone line, whether God or grandma, could speak to you and to you alone. Waves belong to the magic or angelic otherworld; wires knit us tightly into this one. Waves are expansively, inclusively utopian; wires are suspiciously conspiratorial (there is no such thing as 'wave-tapping').

The current return of the dream of 'wireless' connection and communication has to contend with the fact that, by the end of the twentieth century, the word 'wireless' had itself developed a very antique aroma, conjuring up associations of crystal radios, Glenn Miller and Churchillian broadcasts to the nation. When I think of the word 'wireless', I think, not of the newly immaterial world of virtual, or out-of-the-body, experience opening up for us once again, but of a vast, mythical apparatus, the wireless which occupied most of our rather cramped council house living room in the 1960s. I remember it mostly as a thing of textures; the dark, glassily polished wood of its frame, that seemed both to solicit and to forbid the smeary, mortal touch of fingers; the bonier, beakish feel of the hard, yellowing plastic knobs; the coarse, hempy roughness of the fabric stretched over the loudspeaker, which would well and gulp and belly as though taking breath when you turned up the bass. And, most of all, the thing I remember about the thing we called our wireless was the electric cable that connected it to the mains: insulated with tough, woven fabric, inside which was a rubber sleeve, which in its turn enclosed the copper wire along which the power passed. I played perilously with this and other wires, razoring through the epidermal layers, laying bare the gleaming copper ore at their hearts, which, being by this ravishment still unsatisfied, I then spread and splayed and plaited.

Nearly everything is much older than we think, including and especially electricity. The word 'electricity' comes from the Greek word for amber which was known to produce sparks when rubbed. Strange and powerful though it is, human beings habituated themselves early to electricity. By the end of the eighteenth century, the effects of electricity on and in the human body were being intensively investigated by curious physicists, such as the Abbé Jean-Antoine Nollet, who memorably performed an experiment to determine the speed of electricity; he joined 200 Carthusian monks into a ring to see how long it took an electric current to get round, and greatly enjoyed the ensuing yelps and spasms: 'It is singular to see the multitude of different gestures, and to hear the instantaneous exclamation of those surprised by the shock'. The Abbé's speciality was bodily electricity, but he was followed by many others who tried to find or imagine ways of taking this new force into the body, often for medical purposes, to invigorate, or to assist healing. But many thought that there was a strong affinity between external and internal forms of electricity; Nollet himself thought that electricity went both outwards and inwards from electrified bodies, alternating 'affluence' and 'effluence' in a sort of breathing pattern.[2]

The nineteenth-century practice of mesmerism, which depended upon the theory of a transmissible animal magnetism, or soul-force, threw up many examples of people starting to conceive of themselves as kinds of electrical apparatus formed by wire-like connections. The inventor of mesmerism, Anton Mesmer, would conduct therapeutic seances, in which the assembled group would join hands to conduct and contain the force. If we sometimes think of wires as the world's nervous system, pulsing with messages and information, then this is amply anticipated in the ways in which human bodies began to be thought of, not as a hydraulic mechanism, but as wired together, and therefore sometimes capable of being rewired. It was believed that mesmeric trance, for example, could bring about a relocation of the sense organs, so that people who became deaf and blind could nevertheless see and hear from their stomachs. An early nineteenth-century investigator called Jacques-Henri Petetin claimed to have demonstrated an electrical basis for this phenomenon; he said that a subject who would show no sign of response to a question directed to her ears would respond if the mesmeriser placed the fingertips of one hand on her abdomen and whispered his remarks to the fingertips of the other hand.[3]

Spiritualist practice inherited from mesmerism the idea of wiring that connected the body to various kinds of imaginary ether. This idea took its most spectacular form in the images of a medium called Mina Stinson Crandon, who was extensively investigated in Boston during the 1920s. 'Margery', as she was known, specialised in producing the voices of her dead brother Walter, sometimes producing for the photographer a rather ghastly looking talking head made of ectoplasm for the purpose. In one remarkable photograph, the ectoplasmic amplifier sits on her head like a caul, while a thin but perfectly visible thread runs into her ear; in others a smaller teleplasmic mass rests on her shoulder, connected to her by a thick cable that runs into her nose.[4] Hearing, speaking, eating, telephoning, excretion and birth are here wired up in a fantastic and grotesque synthesis, as though in an attempt to keep up with the new ways of hooking up bodies with machines in communicative technologies like telephones, phonographs, typewriters, radios and cinema projectors, which were promising and threatening to change the human body's experience of itself.

One of the ways in which human beings seem most literally to be wired to each other is through the umbilical cord, a linking of times as well as places. Stephen Dedalus in Joyce's *Ulysses* imagines a cable knotted together from all the umbilical cords of human beings, that would give you access to the first telephone number: 'The cords of all link back, strandentwining cable of all flesh ... Put me on to Edenville. Aleph, alpha: nought, nought, one'.[5]

If an umbilical cord offers one way of breathing through a wire, the venerable metaphor of the Aeolian harp offers another way of imagining the susceptibility of wires to the action of the breath. This metaphor was sometimes transposed to telegraph and telephone cables, in an effort to link the new and uncanny moaning they made in the wind to the messages they were conveying. In a poem called 'The Telephone Harp' published in 1908, John Payne imagined telephone cables as a harp swept by the 'hand of the storm-wind', which provided a 'concert of wail that comes from other worlds than ours, / The inarticulate cry of things that till now were mute / And speak out their need through the strings of this monstrous man-made lute'.[6]

Wires are magical objects because they are so small, and capable of wreaking effects far disproportionate to their size and fragility. Human beings are captivated by the idea of infinite force moving through near-infinite littleness. Wires effect transformation, carry messages and impulses. They bring the world to life; they transmit sentience itself. The life that wires transmit passes into them: all wires are live wires, they are all life forms. In my childhood home, we always, superstitiously, unplugged all our electrical apparatus during thunderstorms, in an acknowledgement that our domestic wiring hooked us up to the skies. Lightning, which can turn anything into a conductor, seems to be the confirmation that nature craves the chance to disclose its hidden wirings. Wires not only transform the things they connect, they are themselves subject to all kinds of imaginary collusion and metamorphosis. Wires are like threads, like pipes, like nerves, veins and stems. Dylan Thomas memorably twists together all these ideas in the poem that begins and is titled 'The force that through the green fuse drives the flower'.[7]

We live in a wireless age that has reinvented the wire, as though it continued to put us under some ligatory obligation. We know perfectly well that wires are different from threads and strings and ropes that we can handle, but we seem not to be able to do without the sense of physical involvement with wires. Somebody who turns aside from one mobile phone to take a call from another may still refer to the caller 'on the other line'. When we invite somebody to stay in touch, we are likely to have in mind the special kind of attenuated, arachnid touch involved in contact by wires. Telephones are linked to touching in a way that radio is not: your interlocutor seems still to be at the end of the line, which is perhaps why telephones have retained such surprisingly various erotic possibilities.

Wires, which we will sometimes also call lines, also have the magical power of *the straight*. Although nature everywhere implies and approximates to straight lines – in the force of gravity which pulls a plumb line into verticality, for example – it rarely actually supplies them. Because the idea of the straight is an absolute or counterfactual ideal, straight lines imposed upon nature seem to imply the possibility of magical power. Lines – the lines of architecture and geometry, ley lines, songlines, and the laminar rows imparted by combs – out-nature nature. Lines signify mortality and the irreversibility of time. Wires have the magical property of being able to preserve their inhuman straightness amid convolution. You can knot and wind wires together, but you cannot fold a wire in on itself like clay or dough. The wire retains its linearity through every contortion and insinuation.

Coils, those strange amalgams of the straight and the curved, had always been full of marvel. It is perhaps no surprise that the phonograph, invented almost simultaneously with the telephone, in 1876, should depend upon the principle of coiling, spiralling and winding up, as though it were itself based upon the powers of the wire to compact and store up time. Winding and unwinding continued to be the principles which governed recording and playback when the gramophone record replaced the cylinder-phonograph and persisted in the tape recorder and cine-camera, which turn the line of time into a loop or coil. The neat reversibility of recording and playback is the promise of Ariadne's thread, that will lead us safely out of the labyrinth.

Wires effect their actions very largely invisibly, like our veins and nerves. Whenever and wherever a wire becomes visible, ideas of injury and obscenity stir. A cut or disconnected wire seems dangerous and pitiable at once; something has bitten it, but its wounded condition makes it look menacing, too, as though it were about to bite. The invention of barbed wire, and the use of electric wires for fencing of animals and human beings, made some of this buried threat visible and explicit. This is why, for the most part, wires are so elaborately and decently, as we say, 'clad'; it means that we can be spared the sight and touch of the wire itself, the copper performing its ferocious, invisible and unthinkably rapid business inside the wire.

If wires are life forms, and borrow some of the features of our bodies, they are alien life forms, whose bodies are organised like those of snakes, worms, or other memberless creatures. Wires are venomous, verminous, parasitic parody-life. For me there has always been a peculiar disgust associated with the idea that there really could be a creature called a 'wireworm'. The laying of the transatlantic telephone cable in the nineteenth century was accompanied by much heroic fanfaring, but I think that people may also have been haunted by the idea of that wire lying there, indifferently pervaded by our rages, musings and despairs, out of sight, but never satisfactorily out of mind, slithered over by blind, white things, amid the cold and dark that were its natural element. Wires, like serpents and dragons, belong to unseen, inhospitable, inhuman places; they make our words and impulses and feelings pass through invisibility and uninhabitability. The magic of coils – which associates Faraday's electromagnetic coil with the power invested in amulets showing interwoven forms – is itself tangled up with the peculiar, phobic fascination with the bodies of creatures like snakes capable of coiling over themselves and others of their species, creatures whose singularity is dubious, creatures of the labyrinth whose bodies are themselves labyrinthine. No matter what I do with bits of Sellotape and string, the connections behind my audio system insist on writhing together into this kind of Medusan tangle.

If wires, like pipes, intimate a simplified, abstracted, rationalised world, a world arranged in clean lines and squares, it is in their nature to betray that into convolution; for wires breed on themselves; they seem to touch themselves up, and touch each other off. I comb out the wires at the back of my music system or television so that they hang in a neat and orderly fringe, but when next I pull the unit out, they have coiled and moiled together. They are all middle, heads and tails obscenely muddled. A wired world is the promise of the world recomposed as a vast telephone exchange, in which everything can make contact with everything else, all calls will be returned, and everything will loop magically back on itself; but there was, and is, a vileness that breeds within wires, with their whispers of dropped stitches and disconnections, crossed wires, mazes and black magic.

But, because of this, wires also suggest a thrilling fragility and risk. We depend on them, because our words, and lives, hang on them by a thread. If wires suggest the possibility of binding, they are also closely associated with ideas of hanging on. Callers are asked to 'hold'; the telephone thins our being into a thread. Creatures who hang, like bats, spiders and monkeys, are creatures who live in the worlds of earth and air at once. For all our dreams of flight, we seem to find hanging a more congenial way of occupying the air. The fact that wires are almost not there at all makes them aerial as well as eerie. Our networks of wires, though buried under the ground or even under the ocean, form an imaginary hammock that seems to hold us ecstatically suspended in thin air, even as we go our ways about the earth. During the nineteenth century there were slack-rope and tightrope walkers in the circuses; by the end of the century, they were just as often known as high-wire artists. We had all come to know something of the giddiness of walking on wires. Wires suggest fragility and vertigo, theirs and ours, as well as power. If the connection is cut, if the line goes dead, then we may fall back to earth.

But it is just this tension that keeps us strung out on wires. High-wire walking has become an image of the refinement of the accidents and approximations of human life to the absolute concentration of purpose required to walk the wire. In his essay 'Le funambule' (1958) Jean Genet made the tightrope walker the figure of the solitary, self-communing artist and sexual outsider.

> With his first movements on the wire, we will see that this monster with purple eyelids could dance only there. Doubtless, one will say, it is his singularity which has him balanced on a thread, it is that elongated eye, those painted cheeks, those gilded nails, which oblige him to be there, where we, thank God, would never go.[8]

In August 1974, the high-wire artist Philippe Petit stole into the newly constructed World Trade Center in New York, shot a cable between the buildings with a bow and arrow, and spent 45 minutes walking back and forth between the towers. It seemed to show, as his associate Jean-Louis Blondeau remarked in *Man on Wire* (2008), the documentary film made of the episode, 'what the buildings were for'. This reveals how little Nietzsche really understood about walking the wire when he wrote 'Man is a rope, fastened between animal and Superman – a rope over an abyss ... What is great in man is that he is a bridge and not a goal; what can be loved in man is that he is a *going-across*'.[9] But rope-dancers and wire-walkers do not, any more than chickens, want to get to the other side. In fact, the most characteristic gesture of the wire-walker is, once they have apparently completed their walk safely, to go back out on the wire, as Philippe Petit did for forty-five rapturous, electrifying minutes above the streets of Manhattan, in order to invent different, even more improbably serene things to do on it. Wire-walkers are not heroes but clowns, who offer better company, seem better, as the Americans say, to hang with – 'come on up, come on out, it's lovely!' – than Nietzsche's nobly aquiline souls, perched on high. Like the tap dancer on a staircase, whose task is not to effect a simple ascent or descent, but to come up with as many different ways as possible to combine going up with coming down, the wire-walker aims to occupy rather than merely to penetrate space, to tangle up the line into a cat's-cradle, to dither the infinitesimally thin itinerary of the wire into a five-miles-meandering mazy habitat. The wire-walker wants to persuade us that the perilous wire is in fact a safety net. The destiny of the wire-walker is an indefinite deferral of destination, a putting off of coming to ground. Not an infiltrator but an expatiator, not a courier but a semi-conductor, not a transient but a temporiser, not a metre but a rhythm, the wire-walker offers a joyously perilous set of variations on ways for the performance to be spun out a little longer. The dallying business of the wire-walker is to insinuate a discourse with the wire, forming an amalgam with it of flesh and geometry. For Genet, the role of the wire-walker is to bring his wire to life – 'you will perfect your leaps … not for your own glory, but so that a dead, voiceless steel wire at last may sing'.[10]

When I gave a radio talk on wires in 2000, I was contacted shortly afterwards by the editor of *Wire Industry*, who asked me if I would be willing for them to publish my talk. I wondered quite what he was expecting his readers to get from what I had written. For *Wire Industry* is a trade journal mostly taken up with the technicalities of wires and cables and with wire-related products such as extruders, capstans, stranders and respoolers; it publishes articles with titles like 'Neural Networks for Quality Control in the Wire Rod Industry' and 'The Bending Stiffness of Spiral Strands'. I felt humbled and reproved when I was sent my copy, and found that it was headed with a trail of red hearts fluttering round the caption 'Rekindle Your Love Affair … With Wire'. We should never under-estimate the capacity of human beings to get wound up in things.[11]

Notes

Introduction: Speaking of Objects

1. J. J. Gibson, *The Ecological Approach to Visual Perception* (Hillsdale NJ, Lawrence Erlbaum, 1986), pp.127–46.
2. Gaston Bachelard, *La Terre et les rêveries de la volonté* (Paris, Corti, 1948), p.78.
3. Philip Larkin, *The Whitsun Weddings* (London, Faber and Faber, 1964), p.40.
4. William Shakespeare, *King Lear*, ed. Kenneth Muir (London and New York, Methuen, 1972), II.iv.262–65, p.93.

Bags

1. Jonathan Swift, *Gulliver's Travels*, ed. Paul Turner (Oxford and New York, Oxford University Press, 1986), pp.184–85.
2. John S. Farmer and W. E. Henley, *Slang and its Analogues Past and Present: A Dictionary, Historical and Comparative, of the Heterodox Speech of All*

Classes of Society for More Than Three Hundred Years (7 vols., London, for subscribers, 1903), vol. 1, p.102.

3. Samuel Beckett, *Complete Dramatic Works* (London, Faber and Faber, 1986), pp.25, 28, 29–30.
4. Beckett, *Complete Dramatic Works*, p.151.
5. Isaac Rosenberg, *The Poems and Plays of Isaac Rosenberg*, ed. Vivien Noakes (Oxford and New York, Oxford University Press, 2004), p.140.
6. Farmer and Henley, *Slang*, vol. 1, p.106.
7. Steven Connor, 'Windbags and Skinsongs', online at www.stevenconnor. com/windbags

Batteries

1. Wun Chok Bong, *The Gods' Machines: From Stonehenge to Crop Circles* (Berkeley, Frog Books, 2008), p.84.
2. Marcello Pera, *The Ambiguous Frog: The Galvani-Volta Controversy on Animal Electricity*, trans. Jonathan Mandelbaum (Princeton, Princeton University Press, 1992), pp.83–84.
3. Paola Bertucci, 'Therapeutic Attractions: Early Applications of Electricity to the Art of Healing', *Brain, Mind and Medicine: Essays in Eighteenth-Century Neuroscience*, ed. Harry Whitaker, C. U. M. Smith and Stanley Finger (New York, Springer, 2007), pp.271–83.
4. Arthur Elsenaar and Remko Scha, 'Electric Body Manipulation as Performance Art: A Historical Perspective', *Leonardo Music Journal*, 12 (2002), 17.
5. Georg Mathias Bose, 'Abstract of a Letter from Monsieur De Bozes, Professor of Experimental Philosophy, at the Academy of Wirtemberg, to Monsieur De Maizau', *Philosophical Transactions of the Royal Society of London*, 43 (1745), 419–21.
6. William Watson, 'A Letter from Mr. William Watson, F. R. S. to the Royal Society, Declaring That He as Well as Many Others Have Not Been Able to Make Odours Pass Thro' Glass By Means of Electricity; and Giving a Particular Account of Professor Bose at Wittemberg His Experiment of Beatification, or Causing a Glory to Appear Round a Man's Head By

Electricity', *Philosophical Transactions of the Royal Society of London*, 46 (1749), 351–52.

7. Marco Piccolino, 'The Taming of the Electric Ray: From a Wonderful and Dreadful "Art" to "Animal Electricity" and "Electric Battery"', *Brain, Mind and Medicine: Essays in Eighteenth-Century Neuroscience*, ed. Whitaker, pp.125–43.

8. Alessandro Volta, 'On the Electricity Excited by the Mere Contact of Conducting Substances of Different Kinds', *Philosophical Transactions of the Royal Society of London*, 90 (1800), 403–31.

9. Wilhelm König, 'Ein galvanisches Element aus der Partherzeit?', *Forschungen und Fortschritte*, 14 (1938), 8–9.

10. Paul Keyser, 'The Purpose of the Parthian Galvanic Cells: A First-Century A.D. Electric Battery Used For Analgesia', *Journal of Near Eastern Studies*, 52 (1993), 81–98.

11. Volta, 'On the Electricity Excited', 405, 419 [author's translation].

12. Joost Meertens, 'Shocks and Sparks: The Volatic Pile as a Demonstration Device', *Isis*, 89 (1998), 300–11.

13. Volta, 'On the Electricity Excited', 403.

14. Giuliano Pancaldi, *Volta: Science and Culture in the Age of Enlightenment* (Princeton and Oxford, Princeton University Press, 2003), p.276.

15. Marco Piccolino, 'The Taming of the Electric Ray', pp.125–43.

16. Bern Dibner, *Alessandro Volta and the Electric Battery* (New York, Franklin Watts, 1964), p.79.

17. J. O. N. Rutter, *Human Electricity: The Means of Its Development, Illustrated By Experiments* (London, John W. Parker and Son, 1854), pp.112, 46, 167.

18. Benjamin Brodie, *Psychological Inquiries: In a Series of Essays, Intended to Illustrate the Mutual Relations of the Physical Organization and the Mental Faculties* (London, Longman, Brown, Green and Longmans, 1854), p.156.

19. Herbert Tibbits, *How to Use a Galvanic Battery in Medicine and Surgery: A Discourse Upon Electro-Therapeutics Delivered Before the Hunterian Society Upon November 8th, 1876* (London, J. and A. Churchill, 1877).

20. Bob McCoy, *Quack! Tales of Medical Fraud From the Museum of Questionable Medical Devices* (Santa Monica, Santa Monica Press, 2000), p.58.

21. H. P. Blavatsky, *Isis Unveiled: A Master-Key to the Mysteries of Ancient and Modern Science and Theology* (2 vols., New York and London, J. W. Bouton, 1877), vol. I, p.322.

22. Anna Bonus Kingsford, *'Clothed With the Sun'. Being the Book of the Illuminations of Anna Bonus Kingsford*, ed. Edward Maitland (London, John M. Watkins, 1889), pp.58–59.

23. 'Yogi Ramacharaka' (William Walker Atkinson), *The Hindu-Yogi Science of Breath: A Complete Manual of the Oriental Breathing Philosophy of Physical, Mental, Psychic and Spiritual Development* (Chicago, Yogi Publication Society, 1903), p.21.

24. 'Magus Incognito' (William Walker Atkinson), *The Secret Doctrine of the Rosicrucians* (London, L. N. Fowler, 1918), pp.58–59.

25. Soyen Shaku, *Sermons of a Buddhist Abbot*, trans. Daisetz Teitaro Suzuki (Chicago, Open Court, 1906), p.152.

26. Upton Sinclair, *Mental Radio* (New York, Albert and Charles Boni, 1930), p.213.

27. Alexander McAdie, 'The Storage Battery of the Air', *Harper's New Monthly Magazine*, 89 (1894), 216–19.

28. Richard Schallenberg, *Bottled Energy: Electrical Engineering and the Evolution of Chemical Energy Storage* (Philadelphia, American Philosophical Society, 1982), pp.190–91, 250–322.

Buttons

1. Valerie Steele, ed., *Encyclopaedia of Clothing and Fashion* (3 vols., Detroit, Thomson Gale, 2005), vol. 1, p.209.

2. John S. Farmer and W. E. Henley, *Slang and its Analogues Past and Present: A Dictionary, Historical and Comparative, of the Heterodox Speech of All Classes of Society for More Than Three Hundred Years* (7 vols., London, for subscribers, 1903), vol. 1, p.256.

3. Randle Cotgrave, *A Dictionarie of the French and English Tongues* (Columbia, University of South Carolina Press, 1968), n.p.

4. James Orchard Halliwell, *A Dictionary of Archaic and Provincial Words, Obsolete Phrases, Proverbs, and Ancient Customs From the Fourteenth Century* (2 vols., London, Reeves and Turner, 1889), vol. 1, p.223; John Florio, *Queen Anna's New World of Words, or Dictionarie of the Italian and English Tongues* (London, Edward Blount and William Barret, 1611), pp.209, 276.

5.   Victor Houart, *Buttons: A Collector's Guide* (London, Souvenir Press, 1977), p.25.

6.   Heritage Coach Company, 'Hearses and Buttons and Other Superstitions', *Heritage Coach Dealer USA Blog*, 8 June 2009, online at: blog.heritagecoach. com/funeral-cars/hearses-and-buttons-and-other-superstitions/

7.   Pele Omori, 'A Guide for the Anxious: 11 Japanese Superstitions for Bad Luck', *Matador Abroad*, 7 September 2009, online at: matadorabroad. com/a-guide-for-the-anxious-11-japanese-superstitions-for-bad-luck/

8.   Michel Serres, *The Parasite*, trans. Lawrence R. Schehr (Minneapolis and London, University of Minnesota Press, 2007), p.227.

9.   Joseph, Wright, ed., *The English Dialect Dictionary* (6 vols., Oxford, Oxford University Press, 1970), vol. 1, p.468.

10. Eric Partridge, *A Dictionary of Slang and Unconventional English*, 8th edn., ed. Paul Beale (London and New York, Routledge, 1984), p.166; Joseph A. Weingarten, *An American Dictionary of Slang and Colloquial Speech* (New York, n.p., 1954), p.52.

11. John Dix, *Lions: Living and Dead; or, Personal Recollections of the 'Great and Gifted'*, 2nd edn. (London, W. Tweedie, 1854), p.29.

12. Edward Moor, *Suffolk Words and Phrases; or, An Attempt to Collect the Local Lingualisms of That County* (Woodbridge, for R. Hunter, 1823), p.377; Robert Ford, *Children's Rhymes, Children's Games, Children's Songs, Children's Stories: A Book for Bairns and Big Folk* (Paisley, Alexander Gardner, 1904), p.21.

13. Iona Opie and Moira Tatem, eds., *A Dictionary of Superstitions* (Oxford and New York, Oxford University Press, 1989), p.51.

14. Farmer and Henley, *Slang*, vol. 1, p.456.

15. Houart, *Buttons*, p.29.

16. H. C. Marshall, *Buttons: Summary of the History and Modern Production* (Berkhamsted, British Button Council, 1978), p.1.

17. Liza Cleland, Glenys Davies and Lloyd Llewellyn-Jones, *Greek and Roman Dress From A to Z* (London and New York, Routledge, 2007), p.26.

18. Steele, ed., *Encyclopaedia of Clothing and Fashion*, vol. 1, p.206.

19. James Robinson Planché, *A Cyclopaedia of Costume or Dictionary of Dress* (2 vols., London, Chatto and Windus, 1876), vol. 1, p.67.

20. Marshall, *Buttons*, p.2.

21. Grace Horney Ford, *The Button Collector's History* (Stratford, CT, New England Publishing Co., 1976), p.9.

22. John Calvin, *The Sermons of M. John Calvin Upon the Fifth Booke of Moses Called Deuteronomie ...*, trans. Arthur Golding (London, for George Bishop, 1583), p.472.

23. Steele, ed., *Encyclopaedia of Clothing and Fashion*, vol. 1, p.206.

24. Tom Dalzell and Terry Victor, eds., *The New Partridge Dictionary of Slang and Unconventional English* (2 vols., London and New York, Routledge, 2006), vol. 1, p.319.

25. Partridge, *A Dictionary of Slang*, p.167.

26. E. H. Pearce, *Annals of Christ's Hospital* (London, Methuen and Co., 1901), p.186.

Cards

1. Edwin S. Abbott, *Flatland: A Romance of Many Dimensions*, ed. Thomas Banchoff (Princeton, Princeton University Press, 1991).

2. William James, *Essays on Radical Empiricism* (Lincoln and London, University of Nebraska Press, 1996), p.86.

3. Lars Heide, *Punched-Card Systems and the Early Information Explosion 1880–1945* (Baltimore, Johns Hopkins University Press, 2009).

4. Ambrose Heal, 'Samuel Pepys His Trade-Cards', *The Connoisseur*, 92 (1933), 165–71.

5. Robert Jay, *The Trade Card in Nineteenth-Century America* (Columbia, University of Missouri Press, 1987), p.4.

6. Margaret E. Hale, 'The Nineteenth-Century American Trade Card', *Business History Review*, 74 (2000), 684.

7. Jay, *The Trade Card*, p.99.

8. Roy Genders, *A Guide to Collecting Trade and Cigarette Cards* (London, Pelham Books, 1975), p.30.

9. London Cigarette Card Company, *The Complete Catalogue of British Cigarette Cards* (Exeter, Webb and Bower, 1981), pp.28, 9.

10. Brendan C. Boyd and Fred C. Harris, *The Great American Baseball Card Flipping, Trading, and Bubble Gum Book* (Boston, Little, Brown, 1973), pp.11–12.

11. Michael O'Keeffe and Teri Thompson, *The Card: Collectors, Con Men, and the True Story of History's Most Desired Baseball Card* (New York, HarperCollins, 2007).

12. William Shakespeare, *King Henry V*, ed. Andrew Gurr (Cambridge, Cambridge University Press, 1992), III.i.7, p.117.

13. Edward Bellamy, *Looking Backward 2000–1887* (Boston, Houghton Mifflin, 1941), p.68.

14. Lewis Carroll, *The Annotated Alice: Alice's Adventures in Wonderland and Through the Looking-Glass*, ed. Martin Gardner (Harmondsworth, Penguin, 1970), p.161.

15. Joseph Murphy, *How to Pray With a Deck of Cards* (Los Angeles, Mel Cobb, 1974), pp.7–8.

16. Austin Osman Spare, *Two Tracts on Cartomancy* (London, Fulgur, 1997), pp.27–29.

17. John S. Farmer and W. E. Henley, *Slang and its Analogues Past and Present: A Dictionary, Historical and Comparative, of the Heterodox Speech of All Classes of Society for More Than Three Hundred Years* (7 vols., London, for subscribers, 1903), vol. 6, p.227.

18. Eric Partridge, *The Routledge Dictionary of Historical Slang* (London, Routledge and Kegan Paul, 1973), p.850.

19. Jeremy Collier, *An Essay Upon Gaming, in a Dialogue Between Callimachus and Dolomedes* (London, for J. Morphew, 1713), p.24.

20. Cyril Hughes Hartmann, ed., *Games and Gamesters of the Restoration* (London, Routledge and Sons, 1930), p.xvi.

Combs

1. Walter E. Roth, *An Inquiry into the Animism and Folk-Lore of the Guiana Indians* (Washington, Smithsonian Institute, 1915), p.312.

2. Clement of Alexandria, 'The Instructor', *The Ante-Nicene Fathers: Translations of the Writings of the Fathers Down to A.D. 325: Vol. 2: Fathers of the Second Century: Hermas, Tatian, Athenagoras, Theophilus and Clement of Alexandria*, eds. Alexander Roberts, James Robertson and A. Cleveland Coxe (Grand Rapids, MI, W. B. Erdmans Publishing Co., 1956), p.275.

3. L. S. Rigg et. al., 'The Role of Cloud Combing and Shading by Isolated Trees in the Succession from Maquis to Rain Forest in New Caledonia', *Biotropica*, 34 (2002), 199–210.

4. Bernard Thierry, 'Hair Grows to Be Cut', *Evolutionary Anthropology*, 14 (2005), 5.

5. Alison Jolly, 'Hair Signals', *Evolutionary Anthropology*, 14 (2005), 5.

6. J. G. Frazer, *The Golden Bough: A Study in Magic and Religion* (13 vols., London and Basingstoke, Macmillan, 1990), vol. 3, p.271.

7. M. Tabor, *Chaos and Integrability in Nonlinear Dynamics: An Introduction* (New York, Wiley, 1989), p.187.

8. Patricia Lysaght, 'The Banshee's Comb (MLSIT 4026): The Role of Tellers and Audiences in the Shaping of Redactions and Variations', *Béaloideas*, 59 (1991), 67–82.

9. George Forrest Browne, *Alcuin of York: Lectures Delivered in the Cathedral Church of Bristol in 1907 and 1908* (London, Society for Promoting Christian Knowledge, 1908), pp.49–50.

10. Chih-Hao Li, 'A Laser Frequency Comb That Enables Radial Velocity Measurements With a Precision of 1 cm s^{-1}', *Nature*, 452 (3 April 2008), 610–12.

11. Emily Dickinson, *The Complete Poems*, ed. Thomas H. Johnson (London, Faber and Faber, 1970), p.151.

12. David William Cohen *The Combing of History* (Chicago, Chicago University Press, 1994), p.22.

13. Earl F. Schrock Jr., 'Comb's Getting Red', *Western Folklore*, 31, (1972), 26.

14. Franz Kafka, 'In the Penal Settlement', *Metamorphosis and Other Stories*, trans. Edwin and Willa Muir (Harmondsworth, Penguin, 1970), pp.167–99.

15. Anon, *A Pleasant New Ballad To Sing Both Even and Morne, of the Bloody Murther of Sir John Barley-corne* ... (London, for H.G., 1625).

16. Anon, 'Explosive Hair Combs', *British Medical Journal*, 2 (1897), 1741.

17. Wallace Stevens, *Collected Poems* (London, Faber and Faber, 1984), p.240.

18. Paul Sorrell, 'Alcuin's Comb Riddle', *Neophilologus*, 80 (1996), 311–18.

19. Ernst Dümmler, ed., *Poetae Latini Aevi Carolini I* (Berlin, Weidmann, 1881), p.223 [author's translation].

Glasses

1. Henry James, *The Portrait of a Lady* (Harmondsworth, Penguin, 1971), p.ix.

2. Edward Rosen, 'The Invention of Eyeglasses', *Journal of the History of Medicine and Allied Sciences*, 11 (1956), 13–46, 183–218; Vincent Ilardi, *Renaissance Vision From Spectacles to Telescopes* (Philadelphia, PA, American Philosophical Society, 2007), pp.3–18.

3. Seneca the Younger, *Naturales Quaestiones: With an English Translation By Thomas H. Corcoran* (2 vols., London, William Heinemann; Cambridge, Harvard University Press, 1971), vol. 1, pp.57–59.

4. Tomas Maldonado, 'Taking Eyeglasses Seriously', *Design Issues*, 17 (2001), 32–43.

5. Roger Bacon, *Friar Bacon His Discovery of the Miracles of Art, Nature, and Magick*, trans. T. M. (London, for Simon Miller, 1659), pp.20–21.

6. Pliny the Elder, *Natural History: With An English Translation in Ten Volumes. Volume X: Libri XXXVI–XXXVII*, trans. D. E. Eichholz (London, William Heinemann; Cambridge, Harvard University Press, 1962), XVI.64, 10.215; XVI.63–64, 10.214.

7. Steven Connor, 'Pregnable of Eye: X-Rays, Vision and Magic' (2008), online at www.stevenconnor.com/xray/

8. Anon, 'A Pair of Spectacles', *The Times*, 51225 (10 November 1948), 5.

9. Astrid Vitols, *Dictionnaire des lunettes: historique et symbolique d'un objet culturel* (Paris, Editions Bonneton, 1994), pp.73–79.

10. George H. Oliver, *An Address on the History of the Invention and Discovery of Spectacles* (London, British Medical Association, 1913), p.14.

11. Ilardi, *Renaissance Vision*, p.63.

12. John Donne, *Ignatius His Conclave or His Inthronisation in a Late Election in Hell: Wherein Many Things Are Mingled by Way of Satyr; Concerning the Disposition of Jesuits, the Creation of a New Hell, the Establishing of a Church in the Moone …* (London, for Richard Moore, 1611), pp.4–5.

13. Girolamo Savonarola, *Prediche sopra Ruth e Michea*, ed. Vincenzo Romano (2 vols., Rome, Angelo Belardetti, 1962), vol. 2, pp.379–80, 382 [author's translation].

14. Edgar Allan Poe, 'The Spectacles', *Collected Works of Edgar Allan Poe, vol. 3: Tales and Sketches 1843–1849*, eds. Thomas Ollive Mabbott, Eleanor D. Kewer

and Maureen Mabbott (Cambridge, MA and London, Belknap Press, 1978), pp.883–919.

15. E. T. A. Hoffmann, *The Golden Poet and Other Tales*, trans. Richie Robertson (Oxford, Oxford University Press, 1992), p.105.

16. Arnaud Maillet, *Prothèses lunatiques: les lunettes, de la science aux fantasmes* (Paris, Editions Amsterdam, 2007), p.79.

17. Jean-Paul Sartre, *Being and Nothingness: An Essay On Phenomenological Ontology*, trans. Hazel E. Barnes (London, Methuen, 1984), p.329.

Handkerchiefs

1. George Herbert, *The Complete English Poems*, ed. John Tobin (London, Penguin, 1991), p.104.

2. B.E., *A New Dictionary of the Canting Crew In Its Several Tribes of Gypsies, Beggers, Thieves, Cheats &c.* (London, for W. Hawes etc, 1699).

3. Thomas Rymer, *A Short View of Tragedy Its Original, Excellency and Corruption: With Some Reflections on Shakespear and Other Practitioners for the Stage* (London, Richard Baldwin, 1693), p.138.

4. John Browne, *Adenochoiradelogia, or, An Anatomick-Chirurgical Treatise of Glandules & Strumaes or, Kings-Evil-Swellings: Together With the Royal Gift of Healing, Or Cure Thereof by Contact or Imposition of Hands ...* (London, Tho. Newcomb for Sam. Lowndes, 1684), p.151.

5. Maleeha Lodhi, 'More Talks about Talks', *Daily Mail* (Pakistan), 27 July 2009, online at dailymailnews.com/200907/27/Editorial_Column/DMColumn.php

6. George Chapman, *The Blinde Begger of Alexandria* (London, for William Jones, 1598), sig. B4r.

7. M. Braun-Ronsdorf, *The History of the Handkerchief* (Leigh-on-Sea, F. Lewis, 1967), p.12; George B. Stow, 'Richard II and the Invention of the Pocket Handkerchief', *Albion* 27 (1995), p.226.

8. Braun-Ronsdorf, *The History of the Handkerchief*, p.27.

9. Norbert Elias, *The Civilizing Process: Sociogenetic and Psychogenetic Investigations*, trans. Edmund Jephcott; Eric Dunning, Johan Goudsblom and Stephen Mennell, eds. (Oxford, Blackwell, 2000).

10. Giovanni Della Casa, *Galateo ... Or rather, A treatise of the ma[n]ners and behauiours, it behoueth a man to vse and eschewe, in his familiar conuersation*, trans. Robert Peterson (London, for Raufe Newbery, 1576), p.8.

11. Michel Serres and Bruno Latour, *Conversations on Science, Culture, and Time*, trans. Roxanne Lapidus (Ann Arbor, University of Michigan Press, 1995), pp.60–61.

Keys

1. Craig Raine, *The Onion, Memory* (Oxford, Oxford University Press, 1978), p.62.

2. Thomas Hood, *The Works of Thomas Hood* (7 vols., London, Edward Moxon, 1862–63), vol. 7, p.412.

3. Jean-Paul Sartre, *Being and Nothingness: An Essay On Phenomenological Ontology*, trans. Hazel E. Barnes (London, Methuen, 1984), pp. 259, 260.

4. Gertrude Jobes, *Dictionary of Mythology, Folklore and Symbols* (New York, Scarecrow Press, 1962), p.921.

5. Reginald Scot, *The Discoverie of Witchcraft* (London, for William Brome, 1584), p.477.

6. Lucretius (Titus Lucretius Carus), *On the Nature of the Universe*, trans. R. E. Latham (Harmondsworth, Penguin, 1994), p.48.

7. Jean Chevalier and Alain Gheerbrant, *Dictionnaire des symboles: mythes, rêves, coutumes, gestes, formes, figures, couleurs, nombres* (Paris, Robert Laffont/Jupiter; Chicago, Open Court Publishing Co., 1982), p.261.

8. Jobes, *Dictionary of Mythology*, pp. 920–21.

9. William Shakespeare, *King Richard III*, ed. Anthony Hammond (London, Routledge, 1988), I.ii.5, p.136.

10. Ernest Jones, *Sigmund Freud: Life and Work. Volume One: The Young Freud 1856–1900* (London, Hogarth, 1972), p.139.

11. Dylan Thomas, *The Poems*, ed. Daniel Jones (London, J. M. Dent, 1978), p.172.

12. Vincent Stuckey Lean, *Lean's Collecteanea: Proverbs (English and Foreign), Folk Lore and Superstitions, Also Compilations Toward Dictionaries of Proverbial Phrases and Words, Old and Disused* (4 vols., Detroit, Gale, 1969), vol. 2, p.261.

13. Anon, 'Song of the Keys', *Vanity Fair*, 3 (1861), 192.

Knots

1. Gary Urton, 'From Knots to Narratives: Reconstructing the Art of Historical Record Keeping in the Andes from Spanish Transcriptions of Inka Khipus', *Ethnohistory*, 45 (1998), 409–48.

2. Geraldine Pinch, *Magic in Ancient Egypt* (London, British Museum Press, 1994), p.108.

3. Pliny the Elder, *The Historie of the World: Commonly Called, The Naturall Historie of C. Plinius Secundus*, trans. Philémon Holland (2 vols., London, Adam Islip, 1634), vol. 2, p.305.

4. Frank G. Speck, 'A List of Plant Curatives Obtained From the Houma Indians of Louisiana', *Primitive Man*, 14 (1941), p.56.

5. Andrew H. Gordon and Calvin W. Schwabe, *The Quick and the Dead: Biomedical Theory in Ancient Egypt* (Leiden, Brill/Styx, 2004), p.101.

6. James Hastings, ed., *A Dictionary of the Bible* (10 vols., Honolulu, University Press of the Pacific, 2004), vol. 2, p.69.

7. Michael L. Rodkinson, ed., *The Babylonian Talmud* (2 vols., Boston, New Talmud Publishing Co. 1903), vol. 2, p.230.

8. J. G. Frazer, *The Golden Bough: A Study in Magic and Religion* (13 vols., London and Basingstoke, Macmillan, 1990), vol. 3, p.299.

9. John S. Farmer and W. E. Henley, *Slang and its Analogues Past and Present: A Dictionary, Historical and Comparative, of the Heterodox Speech of All Classes of Society for More Than Three Hundred Years* (7 vols., London, for subscribers, 1903), p.130.

10. James I, of England, *Daemonologie In Forme of a Dialogue, Divided Into Three Bookes* (Edinburgh, Robert Waldegrave , 1597), pp.11, 12.

11. Francis James Child, ed., *The English and Scottish Popular Ballads* (5 vols., New York, Dover, 1965), vol. 1, pp.83–85.

12. J. G. Frazer, *The Golden Bough*, vol. 3, p.298.

13. H. W. Garbutt, 'Native Witchcraft and Superstition in South Africa', *Journal of the Royal Anthropological Institute of Great Britain and Ireland*, 39 (1909), 532.

14. John Scheffer, *The History of Lapland Wherein Are Shewed the Original, Manners, Habits, Marriages, Conjurations, &c. of That People* (Oxford, George West, 1674), p.58.

15. John Brand, *Observations on Popular Antiquities: Chiefly Illustrating the Origin of Our Vulgar Customs, Ceremonies and Superstitions* (2 vols., London, F. C. and D. Rivington, etc., 1813), vol. 2, p.41.

16. Simon Harrison, 'Smoke Rising from the Villages of the Dead: Seasonal Patterns of Mood in a Papua New Guinea Society', *Journal of the Royal Anthropological Institute*, 7 (2001), 261.

17. John Donne, *The Complete English Poems*, ed. A. J. Smith (London, Penguin, 1980), p.55.

18. William Shakespeare, *Antony and Cleopatra*, ed. John Wilders (London and New York, Routledge, 1995), V.ii.303–04, p.296; V.ii.300–02, p.296.

19. William Shakespeare, *The Merry Wives of Windsor*, ed. H. J. Oliver (London and New York, Methuen, 1979), IV.ii.108–09, p.111.

20. William Thomson, 'On Vortex Atoms', *Philosophical Magazine*, 34 (1867), 15–24.

Newspaper

1. Richard L. Hills, *Papermaking in Britain 1488–1988: A Short History* (London, Athlone Press, 1988), p.47.

2. Steven Connor, 'Michel Serres: The Hard and the Soft' (2009), online at www.stevenconnor.com/hardsoft

3. Philip Larkin, *The Whitsun Weddings* (London, Faber and Faber, 1964), p.27.

4. Nicholson Baker, *Double Fold: Libraries and the Assault on Paper* (London, Vintage, 2002), pp.24–25.

5. Abigail J. Sellen and Richard H. R. Harper, *The Myth of the Paperless Office* (Cambridge, MA and London, MIT Press, 2001), pp.16–18; pp.102–03.

6. T. S. Eliot, *Complete Poems and Plays* (London, Faber and Faber, 1969), p.22.

7. Samuel Beckett, *Molloy. Malone Dies. The Unnamable* (London, Calder and Boyars, 1973), p.30.

8. Richard L. Hills, *Papermaking in Britain* , pp.2, 14.

9. Hills, *Papermaking in Britain*, p.143.

10. Vladimir Nabokov, *Speak, Memory: An Autobiography Revisited* (Harmondsworth, Penguin, 1982), p.205.

11. Maurice Rickards, *The Encyclopedia of Ephemera: A Guide to the Fragmentary Documents of Everyday Life for the Collector, Curator and Historian* (London, British Library, 2000), p.190.

12. James Joyce, *Ulysses: The Corrected Text*, ed. Hans Walter Gabler, (Harmondsworth: Penguin, 1986), p.56.

Pills

1. Felix Folio, *The Hawkers and Street Dealers of the North of England Manufacturing Districts… Being Some Account of Their Dealings, Dodgings, and Doings* (Manchester, Abel Heywood, London: T. W. Grattan, 1858), p.51.

2. Laurence M. V. Totelin, *Hippocratic Recipes: Oral and Written Transmission of Pharmacological Knowledge in Fifth- and Fourth-Century Greece* (Leiden and Boston, Brill, 2009), pp.64–66.

3. David Gentilcore, *Medical Charlatanism in Early Modern Italy* (Oxford, Oxford University Press, 2006), p.226.

4. Roy Porter, *Quacks: Fakers and Charlatans in English Medicine* (Stroud, Tempus, 2000), p.50.

5. Sjaak van der Geest and Susan Reynolds Whyte, 'The Charm of Medicines: Metaphors and Metonyms', *Medical Anthropology Quarterly*, 3 (1989), 348–49.

6. Stuart Anderson, 'From "Bespoke" to "Off-the-Peg": Community Pharmacists and the Retailing of Medicines in Great Britain 1900–1970', *From Physick to Pharmacology: Five Hundred Years of British Drug Retailing* (Aldershot and Burlington, VT, Ashgate, 2006), p.129.

7. Morris A. Bealle, *Super Drug Story: A Factological History of America's $10,000,000,000 Drug Cartel – Its Methods, Operations, Hidden Ownership, Profits and Terrific Impact on the Health of the American People* (Washington DC, Columbia Publishing Co., 1962), pp.232, 235.

8. William H. Helfand, 'James Morison and His Pills: A Study of the Nineteenth-Century Pharmaceutical Market', *Transactions of the British Society for the History of Pharmacy*, 1 (1974), 105–06.

9. William H. Helfand, *Quack, Quack, Quack: The Sellers of Nostrums in Prints, Posters, Ephemera and Books: An Exhibition on the Frequently Excessive and Flamboyant Seller of Nostrums as Shown in Prints, Posters, Caricatures, Books, Pamphlets, Advertisements and Other Graphic Arts Over the Last Five Centuries* (New York, The Grolier Club, 2002), fig VI, p.134; Roy Porter, *Quacks*, plates 9 to 16.

10. Sjaak van der Geest and Susan Reynolds Whyte, 'The Charm of Medicines', p.352.

11. Richard Armour, 'Just For the Record,' *Journal of the American Medical Association*, 220 (1972), 92–3.

12. Felix Folio, *The Hawkers and Street Dealers*, p.61.

13. P. S. Brown, 'Female Pills and the Reputation of Iron as an Abortifacient', *Medical History* 21 (1977), 291–304.

14. Francis Burdett Courtenay, *Revelations of Quacks and Quackery: A Series of Letters by 'Detector,' Reprinted from 'The Medical Circular'*, 7th edn. (London, Baillière, Tindall and Cox, 1877), preface to the seventh edition, n.p.

15. Kurt Schapira, H. A. McClelland, N. R. Griffiths, and D. J. Newell, 'Study on the Effects of Tablet Colour in the Treatment of Anxiety States', *British Medical Journal*, 2.5707 (May 23, 1970), 446–49.

16. A. B. A. Overgaard, J. Møller-Sonnergaard, L. L. Christrup, J. Højsted and R. Hansen, 'Patients' Evaluation of Shape, Size and Colour of Solid Dosage Forms', *Pharmacy World and Science*, 23 (2001), 185–88.

17. Barbara Dolinska, 'Empirical Investigation Into Placebo Effectiveness', *Irish Journal of Psychological Medicine*, 16 (1999), 57–58.

Pins

1. Christopher Morley, *Safety Pins and Other Essays* (London, Jonathan Cape, 1925), p.80.

2. Richard Morton and Philip Braham, *Pins: Song* (London, Ascherberg, Hopwood & Crew; New York, T. B. Harms, 1908), p.7.

3. Anon, 'Philosophical Inquiry', *Punch*, 3 (1842), 227.

4. Mary C. Baudry, *Findings: The Material Culture of Needlework and Sewing* (New Haven and London, Yale University Press, 2006), pp.14, 16.

5. E. D. Longman and S. Loch, *Pins and Pincushions* (London, Longmans, Green and Co., 1911), p.20.

6. Anon, *Much a-do about nothing a song made of nothing, the newest in print, he that seriously minds it, shall find all-things in't* (London, for T. Vere, 1660).

7. William Cowper, *The Works of William Cowper*, ed. Robert Southey (15 vols., London, Baldwin and Cradock, 1835–37), vol. 10, p.116.

8. Emanuel Strauss, ed., *Dictionary of European Proverbs* (3 vols., London and New York, Routledge, 1994), vol. 1, p.261.

9. Adam Smith, *An Inquiry Into the Nature and Causes of the Wealth of Nations: A Selected Edition*, ed. Kathryn Sutherland (Oxford, Oxford University Press, 1988), pp.12–13.

10. St Thomas Aquinas, *Summa Theologiae: Latin Text and English Translation, vol. 9: Angels*, ed. and trans. Kenelm Foster (London, Blackfriars, Eyre and Spottiswoode; New York, McGraw-Hill, 1968), I.52.2, 48 [author's translation].

11. Judy Siegel, 'Book of Books Goes Under the Microscope. Technion Prints nano-Bible on Sugar Crystal-Sized Silicon Chip', *Jerusalem Post*, 7 (18 December, 2007).

12. Anon, *Strange and wonderful news from Yowel in Surry giving a true and just account of one Elizabeth Burgiss, who was most strangely bewitched and tortured at a sad rate, having several great lumps of clay pulled forth from her back, full of pins and thorns, which pricked so extreamly that she cry'd and roar'd in a vehement and out-ragious manner, to the great amazement of all the beholders* (London, for J. Clarke, 1681), p.3.

13. Richard Baxter, *The Certainty of the Worlds of Spirits: Fully Evinced By Unquestionable Histories of Apparitions and Witchcrafts* ... (London, for Parkhurst, 1691), p.74.

14. William Shakespeare, *Hamlet*, ed. G. R. Hibbard (Oxford, Oxford University Press, 1998), III.i.76–77, p.241.

15. Herodotus, *The Histories*, trans. Aubrey de Sélincourt, rev. John Marincola (London, Penguin, 2003), pp.87–88, pp.343–44.

16. T. S. Eliot, *Complete Poems and Plays* (London, Faber and Faber, 1969), p.14.

17. Iona Opie and Moira Tatem, eds., *A Dictionary of Superstitions* (Oxford and New York, Oxford University Press, 1989), pp.311–12.

18. James Joyce, *Ulysses: The Corrected Text*, ed. Hans Walter Gabler (Harmondsworth, Penguin, 1986), p.138.

19. Edwin and Mona A. Radford, *Encyclopaedia of Superstitions* (London and New York, Rider, 1948), p.190.

20. Edward Peacock, 'Easter Sunday Superstitions', *Notes and Queries*, series 2, no. 21 (1856), 415.

21. Ad De Vries, *Dictionary of Symbols and Imagery* (Amsterdam and London, North Holland Publishing Co., 1974), p.367.

22. Longman and Loch, *Pins and Pincushions*, p.30.

23. Jacques Fontaine, *Discours des marques des sorciers et de la réelle possession que le diable prend sur le corps des hommes, sur le subiect du procès de l'abominable & detestable sorcier Louys Gaufridy* (Lyon, 1611, n.p.).

24. Longman and Loch, *Pins and Pincushions,* p.48.

25. De Vries, *Dictionary of Symbols and Imagery*, p.367.

26. Eric Grabart and Gay Pauley, 'Milliners' Superstitions', *Western Folklore*, 24 (1965), 120.

27. Opie and Tatem, eds., *A Dictionary of Superstitions*, p.312.

28. James Bonwick, *Irish Druids And Old Irish Religions* (London, Griffith, Farran, 1894), p.243.

29. Gerald Cockshut, arr., *A Paper of Pins* (London, Alfred Lengnick and Co., 1960); Frederic N. Löhr and Frederic A. Weatherley, *Needles and Pins* (London, Patey and Willis, 1890).

30. William Shakespeare, *The Tragedy of Macbeth*, ed. Nicholas Brooke (Oxford, Oxford University Press), IV.i.59–60, p.172.

31. T. J., 'Charm For Warts', *Notes and Queries*, series 1, vol. 7 (1853), 81.

32. Cora Linn Daniels and C. M. Stevans, *Encyclopaedia of Superstitions, Folklore, and the Occult Sciences of the World* (3 vols., Chicago and Milwaukee, J. H. Yewdale & Sons, 1903), vol. 1, p.483.

33. Harry Petroski, *The Evolution of Useful Things* (New York, Alfred A. Knopf, 1993), p.51.

34. Emma M. Stirling, *The History of a Pin* (Edinburgh, Alexander Strahan and Co., London, Hamilton, Adams and Co., 1861), p.3.

35. Christopher Morley, *Safety Pins and Other Essays* (London, Jonathan Cape, 1925), p.81.

36. Hans Christian Andersen, *Andersen's Fairy Tales*, trans. Pat Shaw Iversen (New York, Signet, 2005), p.188.

Pipes

1. Anon, 'Pipes, By A Lover of the Weed', *Bentley's Miscellany*, ii (1842), 493.
2. Anon, 'Pipes', 495–96.
3. Anon, 'Pipes', 494.
4. Arthur Conan Doyle, *The Penguin Complete Sherlock Holmes* (London, Penguin, 1981), p.240.
5. Charles Dickens, *The Mystery of Edwin Drood*, ed. Steven Connor (London, J. M. Dent, 1996), pp.3, 5, 6.
6. Tim Brook, 'Smoking in Imperial China', *Smoke: A Global History of Smoking*, ed. Sander L. Gilman and Zhou Xun (London, Reaktion, 2004), p.88.

Plugs

1. John Bunyan, *A Holy Life, The Beauty of Christianity, or, An Exhortation to Christians to be Holy* (London, for Benjamin Alsop, 1684), p.116.
2. William Shakespeare, *Hamlet*, ed. G. R. Hibbard (Oxford, Oxford University Press, 1998), V.i.194–204, p.330.
3. John Donne, *The Complete English Poems*, ed. A. J. Smith (London, Penguin, 1980), p.60.

Rubber Bands

1. John Bain, 'Recordball.com: Home of the World's Largest Rubber Band Ball' (2008), online at www.recordball.com
2. Thomas Burnet, *The Theory of the Earth* (London, for Walter Kettilby, 1697), p.146.
3. P. G. Tait and W. J. Steele, *A Treatise on the Dynamics of a Particle*, 2nd edn. (Cambridge, Macmillan, 1865), p.288.
4. Robert Boyle, *New Experiments Physico-Mechanical, Touching the Spring of the Air and Its Effects*, *The Works of Robert Boyle: vol 1*, ed. Michael Hunter and Edward B. Davis (London, Pickering and Chatto, 1999), pp.167, 174, 176, 255.

5. James Collins, 'On India-Rubber, Its History, Commerce, and Supply', *Journal of the Society of Arts*, 18 (1869), 81.

6. Francisco Xavier Clavigero, *The History of Mexico*, trans. Charles Cullen (2 vols., London, G. G. J. and J. Robinson, 1787), vol. 1, p.403.

7. Joseph Priestley, *A Familiar Introduction to the Theory and Practice of Perspective* (London, J. Johnson and J. Payne, 1770), p.xv.

8. Leonard MacNally, *Fashionable Levities: A Comedy in Five Acts* (London, G. G. J. and J. Robinson, 1785), p.52.

9. Abbot Lawrence Rotch, 'Benjamin Franklin and the First Balloons', *Proceedings of the American Antiquarian Society*, N. S.18 (1906), 260.

10. Thomas Hancock, *Personal Narrative of the Origin and Progress of the Caoutchouc or India-Rubber Manufacture in England* (London, Longman, Brown, Green, Longmans & Roberts, 1857), pp.3–4, 48–50.

11. Bracy Clark, *A Description of a New Horse Shoe Which Expands to the Foot* (London, for the Author, 1820).

12. James Parton, 'Charles Goodyear', *North American Review*, 101 (1865), 66.

13. Hancock, *Personal Narrative*, p.114.

14. Anon, 'Caoutchouc', *Trewman's Exeter Flying Post or Plymouth and Cornish Advertiser*, 4411 (June 20, 1850), 6.

15. Elizabeth Gaskell, *Cranford*, ed. Elizabeth Porges Watson (Oxford, Oxford University Press, 1998), p.83.

16. Grant Allen, 'The Cinderella of Civilisation', *Longman's Magazine*, 24 (1894), 495.

17. Augustus De Morgan, 'India Rubber', *Notes and Queries*, series 2, vol. 12 (October 26, 1861), 339.

18. Peter Mason, *Cauchu The Weeping Wood: A History of Rubber* (Sydney, Australian Broadcasting Co., 1979), pp. 34–35; John Loadman, *Tears of the Tree: The Story of Rubber – A Modern Marvel* (Oxford, Oxford University Press, 2005), pp.81–107.

19. Thomas Haynes Bayly, *Erin and Other Poems* (Dublin, Richard Milliken; London, Longman, Hurst, and Co., 1822), p.18.

20. 'Young Cuttle', 'Notes on Keeping Notes', *Notes and Queries*, series 1, vol. 10, no. 260 (October 21, 1854), 317.

21. Allen, 'The Cinderella of Civilisation' (1894), p.494.

22. Janet Phillips and Peter Phillips, 'History From Below: Women's Underwear and the Rise of Women's Sport', *Journal of Popular Culture*, 27 (1993), 137–38.

23. William Moore, *The Art of Hair-Dressing, and Making It Grow Fast, Together, With a Plain and Easy Method of Preserving It; With Several Useful Recipes* (London, J. Salmon, 1780), p.39.

24. Auguste Ferry, *Contribution à l'étude de la bande en caoutchouc* [Thèse pour le doctorat en médecine] (Paris, A Paren, 1874).

25. Lillian Whitney, 'Concerning the Teeth', *The Quiver* (April, 1920), 585.

26. Anon, 'Revelations of a Showman', *Blackwood's Edinburgh Magazine*, 77 (1855), 194–95.

27. Anon, 'Anatomical Model', *Belfast News-Letter*, 9707 (June 25, 1830), 4.

28. John Coakley Lettsom, *The Naturalist's and Traveller's Companion, Containing Instructions for Collecting & Preserving Objects of Natural History, and for Promoting Enquiries After Human Knowledge in General* (London, for E. and C. Dilly, 1774), p.87.

29. Maximilian Joseph Lamberg, *Memorial d'un mondain* (2 vols., Paris, n.p., 1776), vol. 1, p.127.

30. Edward B. Foote, *Medical Common Sense; Applied to the Causes, Prevention and Cure of Chronic Diseases and Unhappiness in Marriage* (New York, the Author, 1863), p.380.

31. Friedrich Adolph Wilde, *Das weibliche Gebär-Unvermögen: eine medicinisch-juridische Abhandlung zum Gebrauch practische Geburtshelfer, Aerzte und Juristen* (Berlin, Nicolai'shen Buchhandlung, 1838), p.413; Vincent J. Cirillo, 'Edward Foote's *Medical Common Sense*: An Early American Comment on Birth Control', *Journal of the History of Medicine and Allied Sciences*, 25 (1970), 344–45; Vern L. Bullough, 'A Brief Note on Rubber Technology and Contraception: The Diaphragm and the Condom', *Technology and Culture*, 22 (1981), 105–06.

32. Hancock, *Personal Narrative*, p.14.

33. Allen, 'The Cinderella of Civilisation', pp.492, 494, 496.

34. Anon, 'Mrs Draffen, Corset Maker', *Aberdeen Journal*, 4526 (October 8, 1834), 2.

35. Charles Goodyear, *Gum-Elastic and Its Varieties, With a Detailed Account of Its Applications and Uses, and of the Discovery of Vulcanization* (2 vols., New Haven, for the Author, 1855), p.131.

36. James Parton, 'Charles Goodyear', *North American Review*, 101 (1865), 65, 66.

37. John Gough, 'A Description of a Property of Caoutchouc, or Indian Rubber: With Some Reflections on the Cause of Elasticity of This Substance', *Memoirs of the Literary and Philosophical Society of Manchester*, 2nd series, 1 (1805), 288–95.

38. J. Hartley, *History of the Westminster Election, Containing Every Material Occurrence, From Its Commencement on the First of April, to the Final Close of the Poll, on the 17th of May* (London, J. Debrett, 1784), p.523.

39. 'Vedette', 'Catapult', *Notes and Queries*, series 2, vol. 10 (August 11, 1860), 104.

40. Clavigero, *The History of Mexico*, vol. 1, p.271.

41. Loadman, *Tears of the Tree*, pp.258–76.

42. Leonard Süsskind (2003), 'Interview With John Brockman', *Edge*, online at www.edge.org/3rd_culture/susskind03/susskind_index.html

Sticky Tape

1. Jean-Paul Sartre, *Being and Nothingness: An Essay On Phenomenological Ontology*, trans. Hazel E. Barnes (London, Methuen, 1984), p.67.

2. Merrily A. Smith, Norvell M. M. Jones, II, Susan L. Page and Marian Peck Dirda, 'Pressure-Sensitive Tape and Techniques for Its Removal from Paper', *Journal of the American Institute for Conservation*, 23 (1984), 101–13.

3. John Johnston, *Pressure Sensitive Adhesive Tapes: A Guide to Their Function, Design, Manufacture, and Use* (Northbrook, ILL, Pressure Sensitive Tape Council, 2003), pp.2, 4.

4. W. H. Shecut and Horace H. Day, 'Improvement in Adhesive Plasters', US Patent No. 3956 (March 26, 1845).

5. Virginia Huck, *Brand of the Tartan: The 3M Story* (New York, Appleton-Century-Crofts, 1955), pp.133–34, 135–36, 140–41, 144–45.

6. E. Newton Harvey, 'The Luminescence of Adhesive Tape', *Science*, NS 89 (May 19, 1939), 460–61.

7. Carlos G. Camara, Juan V. Escobar, Jonathan R. Hird and Seth J. Putterman, 'Correlation Between Nanosecond X-ray Flashes and Stick-Slip Friction in Peeling Tape', *Nature*, 455 (23 October 2008), 1089–1092.

Sweets

1. W. B. Yeats, 'Friends', *Collected Poems* (London and Basingstoke, Macmillan, 1979), p.139.
1. Michel Serres, *The Five Senses: A Philosophy of Mingled Bodies (I)*, trans. Margaret Sankey and Peter Cowley (London, Continuum, 2008).

Wires

1. E. M. Forster, *Howards End* (Harmondsworth, Penguin, 1980), p.188.
2. J. L. Heilbron, *Electricity in the 17th and 18th Centuries: A Study of Early Modern Physics* (Berkeley, Los Angeles and London, University of California Press, 1979), p.318.
3. Jacques-Henri-Desiré Petetin, *Électricité animale, prouvée par la découverte des phénomènes physiques et moraux de la catalepsie hystérique, et de ses variétés: et par les bons effets de l'électricité artificielle dans le traitement de ces maladies* (Paris, chez Brunot-Labbe and Gautier and Bretin; Lyon, chez Reyman and Co., 1808), pp.1–17.
4. Malcolm J. Bird, *The Margery Mediumship: A Complete Record From January 1st, 1925* (New York, American Society for Psychical Research, 1928), facing p.226.
5. James Joyce, *Ulysses: The Corrected Text*, ed. Hans Walter Gabler (Harmondsworth, Penguin, 1986), p.32.
6. John Payne, 'The Telephone Harp', *Carol and Cadence: New Poems 1902–1907* (London, Villon Society, 1908), p.96.
7. Dylan Thomas, *The Poems*, ed. Daniel Jones (London, J. M. Dent, 1978), p.73.
8. Jean Genet, 'Le funambule', *Oeuvres complètes*, vol. 5 (Paris, Gallimard, 1979), p.16 [author's translation].
9. Friedrich Nietzsche, *Thus Spoke Zarathustra: A Book for Everyone and No One*, trans. R. J. Hollingdale (Harmondsworth, Penguin, 2003), pp.43–44.

10. Genet, 'Le funambule', p.10.
11. Steven Connor, 'Rekindle Your Love Affair ... With Wire', *Wire Industry*, 67 (2000), 143–46.

Index